# Azure Data Demystified: From SQL to Synapse

Kameron Hussain and Frahaan Hussain

Published by Sonar Publishing, 2025.

AZURE DATA DEMYSTIFIED: FROM SQL TO SYNAPSE

**First edition. April 27, 2025.**



ISBN: 979-8231136827

Written by Kameron Hussain and Frahaan Hussain.

# Azure Data Demystified: From SQL to Synapse

First Edition

# Preface

The cloud has redefined how organizations think about data—how it's stored, processed, analyzed, and ultimately used to derive value. As we transition further into a data-centric era, the ability to manage vast amounts of data across hybrid and multi-cloud environments becomes both a challenge and an opportunity. Microsoft Azure, with its comprehensive and integrated suite of data services, stands at the forefront of this transformation.

**Azure Data Demystified: From SQL to Synapse** is designed to serve as a foundational resource for anyone—whether you are a student, a data engineer, a business analyst, or an IT professional—looking to understand the core principles and capabilities of Azure's data ecosystem. This book takes a practical, hands-on approach to explaining Azure's vast offerings, from the basics of Azure SQL services to real-time analytics with Stream Analytics and IoT, and further into the world of machine learning with Azure Synapse and Azure ML.

Each chapter builds upon the last, gradually guiding readers from introductory topics to more advanced concepts. You'll begin by exploring how Azure structures its data services, then dive deep into specific tools and services like Azure SQL Database, Azure Data Lake Gen2, Azure Synapse Analytics, and Azure Data Factory. We've dedicated space to discuss real-world use cases and industry examples, allowing you to visualize how these technologies come together in practice.

Security, governance, and best practices are not treated as afterthoughts. Instead, they're interwoven into the chapters and then explored in depth in their own dedicated section. As cloud technology continues to evolve, we've also taken the liberty of peeking into the future by discussing AI's growing role, the promise of quantum computing, and how organizations can stay ahead of the innovation curve.

This book is written with clarity and accessibility in mind. Whether you're aiming to pass an exam, lead a cloud migration initiative, or simply enhance your understanding of modern data platforms, this guide is your entry point.

Let's demystify Azure together—one service, one concept, and one practical insight at a time.

# Table of Contents

D

E

F

G

H

I

J

K

L

M

N

O

P

Q

R

S

T

U

V

W

# Chapter 1: Understanding the Azure Data Ecosystem

## Introduction to Cloud-Based Data Platforms

The rapid evolution of cloud computing has revolutionized how organizations store, process, and analyze data. Traditional on-premise infrastructure, once the norm, is increasingly giving way to flexible, scalable, and cost-effective cloud-based solutions. Microsoft Azure, one of the leading cloud service providers, offers a comprehensive suite of tools and services that enable businesses to harness the full potential of their data—regardless of scale or complexity.

### The Paradigm Shift: From On-Premise to Cloud

Historically, data platforms were built in-house. Organizations maintained their own data centers, handled hardware procurement, managed uptime, and dealt with the operational burden of scaling resources manually. This model, while providing a sense of control, was also capital-intensive, slow to scale, and often hindered innovation.

Cloud-based data platforms like Azure have upended this model. With Azure, organizations can provision databases, build data lakes, run analytics workloads, and deploy machine learning models—all with just a few clicks or commands. The cloud introduces agility, elasticity, and democratization of access to powerful tools that were once reserved for tech giants.

Azure's model operates on a **pay-as-you-go** basis, allowing businesses to align costs with usage. This operational expenditure model is often more appealing than the capital expenditure required for on-premise infrastructure. Moreover, Azure's global presence means that data can be stored and processed closer to users, improving performance and compliance.

## Core Benefits of Cloud-Based Data Platforms

Cloud platforms like Azure bring several key advantages:

- **Scalability**: Automatically scale resources up or down based on demand.
- **High Availability**: Built-in redundancy and failover support ensure uptime.
- **Security and Compliance**: Enterprise-grade security features with global compliance certifications.
- **Managed Services**: Focus on insights rather than infrastructure by leveraging PaaS offerings.
- **Integration**: Seamless integration with a broad ecosystem of services including Power BI, Microsoft 365, GitHub, and more.

## Key Azure Data Services at a Glance

Azure offers a vast ecosystem of data services. Some of the foundational components include:

- **Azure SQL Database**: A fully managed relational database service.
- **Azure Data Lake Storage Gen2**: Scalable storage for big data analytics.

- **Azure Synapse Analytics**: An integrated analytics service that brings together big data and data warehousing.

- **Azure Data Factory**: A data integration service for creating ETL/ELT pipelines.

- **Azure Stream Analytics**: A real-time analytics service for stream processing.

- **Azure Machine Learning**: A cloud-based platform for training, deploying, and managing machine learning models.

Each of these services is designed to be modular and interoperable, meaning you can build complex data architectures by combining them as needed.

## Building Blocks of a Modern Cloud Data Platform

Modern cloud data platforms, especially in Azure, are typically composed of the following layers:

1. **Data Ingestion**: Ingest data from diverse sources (on-premise, SaaS apps, IoT devices).
2. **Data Storage**: Store raw and curated data using services like Azure Data Lake and Azure Blob Storage.
3. **Data Processing**: Transform data using Azure Data Factory, Databricks, or Synapse pipelines.
4. **Data Serving**: Store structured data in Azure SQL or Synapse for querying and analysis.
5. **Analytics and AI**: Leverage Synapse, Power BI, or Azure ML to derive insights and build predictive models.
6. **Governance and Security**: Apply RBAC, policies,

auditing, and data lineage with services like Azure Purview.

## Cloud-Native Design Principles

To truly unlock the potential of Azure, it is crucial to design applications and platforms with cloud-native principles:

- **Loose Coupling**: Design services to operate independently.

- **Resilience**: Build systems that gracefully handle failures.

- **Observability**: Integrate monitoring, logging, and alerting from the start.

- **Automation**: Use Infrastructure as Code (IaC) to manage deployments (e.g., ARM templates, Bicep, Terraform).

- **Security First**: Apply Zero Trust principles and encrypt data at rest and in transit.

## Use Cases Driving Cloud Adoption

Across industries, organizations are leveraging Azure's data services to solve complex problems:

- **Retail**: Real-time inventory tracking and personalized customer experiences.

- **Healthcare**: Integration of Electronic Health Records (EHR) with data lakes for better diagnostics.

- **Manufacturing**: IoT-based predictive maintenance and operational analytics.

- **Finance**: Fraud detection and compliance reporting with real-time analytics.

- **Education**: Personalized learning experiences powered by AI and ML.

## Sample Architecture: Data Ingestion to Insight

To put all of this into perspective, let's examine a simplified example of how data flows through an Azure-based platform:

IoT Devices / Web Apps / On-Prem DBs

|

Azure Data Factory

|

Azure Data Lake Storage Gen2 (Raw Layer)

|

Azure Data Factory Mapping Data Flows

|

Azure SQL / Synapse Analytics (Curated Layer)

|

Power BI / Azure ML

In this architecture, data is ingested from various sources into Azure Data Lake Storage. Azure Data Factory orchestrates the transformation and movement of this data into curated stores like Azure SQL or Synapse. From there, analysts and data scientists can use Power BI and Azure ML to derive insights and build models.

## Getting Started with Azure

To begin using Azure's data services, you'll need:

1. **An Azure Account**: Start with a free trial that provides credits.
2. **Azure Portal Access**: The web-based UI to manage services.
3. **Azure CLI / PowerShell**: For scripting and automation.
4. **Resource Group**: A logical container for managing services.
5. **Storage Account**: Basic component for data storage.
6. **Subscription and Cost Controls**: To manage billing and budgets.

Here's a simple example of provisioning a resource group and a SQL database using Azure CLI:

```
# Login to Azure

az login

# Create a resource group

az group create—name azure-data-book—location eastus

# Create a SQL server

az sql server create \

—name azuresqlserver123 \
```

```
—resource-group azure-data-book \

—location eastus \

—admin-user adminuser \

—admin-password StrongP@ssword123

# Create a SQL database

az sql db create \

—name sampledb \

—resource-group azure-data-book \

—server azuresqlserver123 \

—service-objective S0
```

## Final Thoughts

The cloud is more than just a technology shift—it's a cultural and operational transformation. Azure provides a rich set of capabilities to support this evolution. Whether you're dealing with structured databases, big data lakes, streaming IoT data, or advanced analytics with machine learning, Azure equips you with the tools to turn raw data into meaningful action.

This chapter laid the foundation for understanding how the Azure data ecosystem is structured and why it matters. In the next chapter, we'll dive deep into **Azure SQL Services** and explore how you can provision, manage, and optimize SQL-based workloads in the cloud.

# Overview of Azure's Data Services

Microsoft Azure is a robust cloud platform that provides a wide array of services tailored for data professionals, software developers, business analysts, and enterprises of all sizes. With a focus on scalability, flexibility, and integration, Azure's data services empower organizations to manage the full data lifecycle—ingestion, storage, processing, analysis, and governance—all within a unified ecosystem. This section provides a detailed overview of the key services within Azure's data platform, explaining what they do, when to use them, and how they fit together in real-world solutions.

## Categories of Azure Data Services

Azure's data services can be logically grouped into several categories, each targeting a specific phase of the data lifecycle:

1. **Data Storage** – For storing structured, semi-structured, and unstructured data.
2. **Data Ingestion and Integration** – For collecting and orchestrating data from various sources.
3. **Data Processing and Analytics** – For transforming data and performing large-scale analysis.
4. **Business Intelligence and Visualization** – For creating dashboards and reports.
5. **Machine Learning and AI** – For building predictive models and intelligent applications.
6. **Governance and Security** – For ensuring data quality, access control, and compliance.

Let's explore each of these in depth.

## Data Storage Services

### Azure Blob Storage

Azure Blob Storage is Microsoft's object storage solution optimized for the cloud. It's ideal for storing massive amounts of unstructured data such as text files, images, videos, and backups.

Key features:

- Tiered storage: Hot, Cool, and Archive tiers for cost optimization.
- Lifecycle policies to automatically transition blobs between tiers.
- Secure access via shared access signatures (SAS), managed identities, or keys.

Use case example: Storing raw logs, documents, or video files collected from IoT devices.

### Azure Data Lake Storage Gen2

This is an evolution of Azure Blob Storage, optimized for big data analytics. It provides hierarchical namespace support, fine-grained access control, and high throughput for analytic workloads.

Key benefits:

- Seamless integration with analytics tools like Azure Synapse and Databricks.
- POSIX-style ACLs for security and access control.

- High-performance parallel processing for batch workloads.

Example: A retailer storing years of transactional and customer data for analysis using Spark.

**Azure SQL Database**

Azure SQL Database is a fully managed relational database-as-a-service (DBaaS) based on the Microsoft SQL Server engine. It supports transactional systems, reporting, and hybrid data models.

Core capabilities:

- Automatic backups and patching.
- Built-in high availability and scalability.
- Integration with Azure Monitor and Defender for threat detection.

**Cosmos DB**

Azure Cosmos DB is a globally distributed, multi-model NoSQL database service designed for low-latency, high-throughput workloads.

Supported models:

- Document (Core API)
- Graph (Gremlin)
- Column-family (Cassandra)

- Key-value (Table API)

It allows for:

- Global distribution with single-digit millisecond latency.
- Multi-master replication for high availability.
- Tunable consistency levels.

Used in scenarios requiring geo-distribution, such as mobile apps and online games.

## Data Ingestion and Integration

### Azure Data Factory

Azure Data Factory (ADF) is a cloud-based ETL (Extract, Transform, Load) and ELT (Extract, Load, Transform) service. It enables you to orchestrate workflows that ingest data from over 100 sources.

Features include:

- Code-free data transformation with Mapping Data Flows.
- Monitoring and logging of data pipelines.
- Triggering based on schedule, events, or manually.

Example: Ingesting CRM data from Salesforce into a data lake for analysis.

### Azure Event Hubs

This is a big data streaming platform and event ingestion service capable of receiving millions of events per second. It acts as the entry point for event-driven architectures.

Common uses:

- IoT telemetry ingestion.
- Clickstream analytics.
- Log aggregation.

It integrates seamlessly with Azure Stream Analytics and Apache Kafka.

### Azure IoT Hub

Designed for managing billions of IoT devices, IoT Hub allows for secure bi-directional communication between IoT applications and the devices they manage.

Example: A smart city application monitoring air quality sensors across various districts.

## Data Processing and Analytics

### Azure Synapse Analytics

Synapse is an integrated analytics service that combines enterprise data warehousing and big data analytics. It unifies querying across SQL-based engines and Apache Spark.

Capabilities:

- On-demand SQL querying (serverless).
- Provisioned pools for predictable performance.
- Integrated with Power BI and Azure Machine Learning.

Use case: A large financial institution aggregating and analyzing transaction data for fraud detection.

**Azure Databricks**

A fast, easy, and collaborative Apache Spark-based analytics platform optimized for Azure. It is used for big data processing and machine learning.

Advantages:

- Interactive notebooks for data exploration.
- Native integration with Data Lake and Azure ML.
- MLflow support for model tracking and deployment.

**Azure Stream Analytics**

A real-time analytics service to process data streams from Event Hubs, IoT Hub, and Blob Storage.

Functions:

- Real-time scoring using ML models.

- Output to Power BI for live dashboards.
- SQL-like query language for transformations.

Example: Monitoring live telemetry from factory sensors to detect equipment failures.

## Business Intelligence and Visualization

### Power BI

While not exclusive to Azure, Power BI integrates deeply with Azure data sources. It allows for self-service and enterprise business intelligence.

Benefits:

- Drag-and-drop dashboard creation.
- Scheduled refresh from Azure SQL, Synapse, and Data Lake.
- Natural language query capabilities.

It supports collaborative reporting and role-based sharing within organizations.

### Azure Analysis Services

This is a fully managed platform-as-a-service (PaaS) that provides enterprise-grade OLAP capabilities. It is used for modeling complex business data.

Supports:

- Tabular models built in Visual Studio.
- Complex DAX expressions for calculations.
- Row-level security and partitioning.

Used to power reports that demand fast querying on multidimensional datasets.

## Machine Learning and AI

### Azure Machine Learning

A platform for building, training, and deploying ML models. Azure ML supports automated ML, no-code designer tools, and custom Python/R model development.

Core features:

- MLOps for model lifecycle management.
- Integration with Jupyter notebooks.
- Pipelines for data prep, training, and scoring.

Example: Creating a churn prediction model using historical customer data stored in Azure SQL.

### Cognitive Services

A suite of pre-trained APIs for vision, speech, language, and decision-making. These can be consumed by applications without requiring custom model training.

Examples:

- Text Analytics API for sentiment analysis.
- Computer Vision API for object detection.
- Translator API for language translation.

**Azure OpenAI Service**

Offers access to advanced generative AI models like GPT through a managed API interface. Enables developers to integrate large language models into applications.

Use cases:

- Generating reports from data summaries.
- Automating customer support with chatbots.
- Enabling natural language data querying.

## Governance, Monitoring, and Security

**Azure Purview**

Azure Purview is a unified data governance service that allows organizations to discover, classify, and manage data assets.

Key capabilities:

- Automated data cataloging.
- Data lineage tracking.
- Sensitive data classification.

Example: Identifying all datasets that contain personally identifiable information (PII) across Azure resources.

**Azure Monitor and Log Analytics**

These services provide metrics and logs for infrastructure and applications.

Highlights:

- Custom dashboards.
- Alerts and autoscale triggers.
- Integration with diagnostic logs and activity tracking.

**Azure Policy and RBAC**

To enforce compliance, organizations can use:

- **Role-Based Access Control (RBAC)**: Define who can access which resource.
- **Azure Policy**: Enforce standards like region restrictions, tagging requirements, and allowed SKUs.

Code example for creating a policy to restrict storage accounts to specific regions:

```
{
"if": {
"not": {
```

```
"field": "location",

"in": ["eastus", "westus"]

}

},

"then": {

"effect": "deny"

}

}
```

## Summary: Building Integrated Solutions

What makes Azure powerful is the ability to seamlessly integrate its services into holistic data solutions. Here's a simplified example of how multiple Azure data services could work together:

- **Azure Data Factory** ingests customer data from various sources.
- **Azure Data Lake Gen2** stores raw and curated datasets.
- **Azure Synapse Analytics** transforms and queries that data for insights.
- **Azure Machine Learning** models customer churn predictions.
- **Power BI** visualizes key trends and KPIs.

- **Azure Purview** ensures data governance across the pipeline.

This modularity and interoperability empower developers and organizations to innovate rapidly, scale efficiently, and meet modern data demands with confidence. As the next chapters dive into individual services, this high-level overview serves as the context for understanding how they all interconnect within the Azure ecosystem.

## Comparing On-Premise and Azure Data Architectures

The shift from on-premise to cloud-based data architectures is one of the most impactful transformations in modern IT. Organizations accustomed to controlling every facet of their data infrastructure are now embracing the flexibility, scalability, and cost-efficiency of cloud platforms like Microsoft Azure. However, this transition is more than a technological upgrade—it's a paradigm shift that redefines how data is stored, secured, processed, and analyzed.

This section presents a detailed comparison between traditional on-premise data architectures and modern cloud-native architectures built using Azure. We'll examine infrastructure components, deployment models, scalability strategies, performance optimization, maintenance, security, and cost structures. Additionally, we'll explore hybrid approaches and migration strategies.

## Infrastructure and Architecture

### On-Premise Infrastructure

In an on-premise model, organizations purchase, install, and manage their own hardware. This includes servers, storage systems, networking equipment, and power/cooling systems. The IT team is responsible for maintaining the infrastructure, applying updates, handling outages, and ensuring security.

Typical components:

- Physical data center
- Rack-mounted servers
- Network-attached storage (NAS) or storage area network (SAN)
- Backup appliances and tapes
- Firewalls, routers, and switches

Architecture is often monolithic or layered, with silos for different business units and applications. Integration is complex and expensive, often relying on middleware solutions.

### Azure Cloud Infrastructure

In Azure, infrastructure is virtualized and offered as services—eliminating the need for physical hardware management. Compute, storage, and networking are provisioned and managed via the Azure Portal, CLI, or Infrastructure as Code (IaC).

Typical Azure equivalents:

- Virtual Machines (VMs) or Azure App Service instead of physical servers
- Azure SQL Database instead of on-prem SQL Server
- Azure Blob or Data Lake instead of NAS/SAN
- Azure Backup and Recovery Vault for business continuity
- Azure Virtual Network and Network Security Groups for networking

Architectures in Azure are modular, microservice-oriented, and can be serverless. Systems are built for failure, and scalability is an architectural principle rather than a post-deployment enhancement.

## Scalability and Elasticity

### On-Premise Scalability

Scaling on-prem systems is capital- and labor-intensive. Adding more capacity requires:

- Procurement and delivery of new hardware
- Physical installation and configuration
- Downtime for integration and testing

Vertical scaling (adding more power to existing systems) is limited by hardware specs, while horizontal scaling (adding more servers) requires load balancing and complex orchestration.

### Azure Scalability

Azure offers near-infinite scalability using horizontal and vertical scaling:

- **Vertical Scaling**: Increase the CPU, RAM, or storage of existing VMs or databases with a few clicks.

- **Horizontal Scaling**: Use Azure Load Balancer, Virtual Machine Scale Sets, or App Services autoscaling to handle more traffic.

Elasticity means resources automatically scale based on demand, using metrics like CPU utilization or queue length. This ensures performance during peak loads and cost savings during idle times.

Example: Autoscaling Azure App Service based on CPU threshold

```
{
"autoscale": {
"rules": [
{
"metricTrigger": {
"metricName": "CPUPercentage",
"operator": "GreaterThan",
"threshold": 70,
"timeGrain": "PT1M",
"statistic": "Average",
```

```
"timeWindow": "PT5M",
"timeAggregation": "Average"
},
"scaleAction": {
"direction": "Increase",
"type": "ChangeCount",
"value": "1",
"cooldown": "PT5M"
}
}
]
}
}
```

## Performance and Reliability

### On-Premise Performance

Performance is limited to the physical capacity of deployed hardware. Once resource limits are hit, users may experience downtime, slow query responses, or failed batch jobs.

Reliability is ensured through redundant hardware, failover systems, and backup generators. High availability requires expensive clustering and manual configuration.

### Azure Performance

Azure leverages distributed systems and geographic redundancy:

- Data can be stored in geographically replicated regions using GRS (Geo-Redundant Storage).
- Azure SQL Database offers automatic failover groups and read replicas.
- Content can be distributed using Azure CDN for global performance.

Additionally, services like Azure Front Door and Traffic Manager help route requests based on lowest latency or user geography, enhancing user experience.

Query performance is enhanced using:

- Index tuning
- Materialized views
- Partitioning
- Resource governance (DTUs and vCores)

Azure Monitor and Application Insights provide real-time performance analytics and alerting.

## Maintenance and Upgrades

### On-Premise Maintenance

Maintenance tasks are frequent and include:

- OS and database patching
- Hardware replacement
- Firmware updates
- Security auditing
- Manual failover tests

Downtime windows are required for updates, which may impact SLAs (Service Level Agreements).

**Azure Maintenance**

Azure services are managed and maintained by Microsoft. Most updates are applied automatically with minimal impact to service availability.

Benefits:

- Zero-downtime patching for services like SQL Database
- Service updates rolled out across multiple regions with high availability
- OS-level updates handled by Microsoft for PaaS services

Users focus on application logic, not infrastructure upkeep. SLA uptime for key services exceeds 99.9%.

## Security and Compliance

### On-Premise Security

Security responsibilities rest entirely on the organization. This includes:

- Network segmentation
- Physical security of the data center
- Antivirus and endpoint protection
- Access control using Active Directory
- Manual vulnerability scanning

Compliance with standards like GDPR, HIPAA, or ISO requires internal audits, documentation, and third-party verification.

### Azure Security

Azure implements a **shared responsibility model**:

- Microsoft is responsible for the infrastructure security of the cloud.
- The user is responsible for the data and configuration within the cloud.

Azure's security features:

- Identity and Access Management using Azure AD
- Role-Based Access Control (RBAC)

- Just-In-Time (JIT) VM Access
- Azure Defender and Sentinel for threat detection
- Azure Key Vault for secrets management

Azure is certified for over 100 compliance standards including:

- ISO/IEC 27001
- HIPAA
- SOC 1/2/3
- FedRAMP
- GDPR

Example: Assigning RBAC in Azure CLI

az role assignment create \

—assignee user@example.com \

—role "Reader" \

—scope /subscriptions/{sub-id}/resourceGroups/my-resource-group

## Cost Models

### On-Premise Cost

Costs are largely **CapEx** (Capital Expenditure), including:

- Data center construction and lease

- Hardware procurement
- Utility costs (power, cooling)
- Staffing for operations and support

This model lacks flexibility. Underutilized hardware still incurs costs, and scaling requires significant financial planning.

**Azure Cost**

Azure uses an **OpEx** (Operational Expenditure) model:

- Pay-as-you-go for compute, storage, and bandwidth
- Reserved instances and hybrid benefits reduce long-term costs
- Scaling down during off-hours reduces consumption

Tools like Azure Cost Management + Billing, Budgets, and Advisor help optimize and forecast cloud costs.

Example: Enabling cost alert via Azure CLI

```
az consumption budget create \
—amount 100 \
—category cost \
—name monthlyBudget \
—resource-group my-resource-group \
—time-grain Monthly \
```

—time-period start=2024-01-01T00:00:00Z end=2024-12-31T00:00:00Z

## Hybrid and Migration Strategies

Not all organizations are ready for a full cloud migration. Azure supports **hybrid architectures**:

- **Azure Arc**: Extend Azure services to on-premises or other cloud providers.
- **Azure Stack**: Run Azure services in on-prem environments.
- **ExpressRoute**: Dedicated network connection between Azure and your data center.
- **Site Recovery**: Disaster recovery as a service (DRaaS) for on-prem VMs.

**Lift and shift** strategies use services like Azure Migrate to move existing workloads with minimal changes.

**Replatforming** (e.g., moving SQL Server to Azure SQL Managed Instance) and **refactoring** (breaking monoliths into microservices) offer deeper optimization benefits over time.

## Summary Comparison Table

| Feature | On-Premise | Azure Cloud |
|---|---|---|
| Ownership | Full (hardware + software) | Microsoft-managed |
| Scalability | Manual, hardware-limited | Automatic, virtually unlimited |
| Maintenance | Manual | Automated |
| Deployment Time | Weeks to months | Minutes to hours |
| Upgrades | Manual, often downtime | Seamless, zero-downtime |
| Cost Model | CapEx | OpEx |
| Security | Organization-driven | Shared responsibility |
| Compliance | Manual audits | Built-in with certifications |
| Disaster Recovery | Costly, complex | Integrated services |
| Elasticity | None | Built-in auto-scaling |

## Final Thoughts

Comparing on-premise and Azure data architectures isn't merely a technical evaluation—it reflects a broader shift in how modern businesses approach agility, innovation, and risk. While on-premise setups offer control and familiarity, Azure offers unparalleled flexibility, performance, and efficiency.

Understanding the differences helps organizations make informed decisions about cloud adoption, architecture design, and operational strategy. Whether you're considering a hybrid approach, planning a cloud migration, or building net-new systems in Azure, embracing this shift is a step toward future-ready data platforms.

In the next section, we'll explore how these architectural principles manifest in key industry use cases and scenarios, providing a lens into how different sectors are leveraging Azure to transform their data-driven operations.

# Key Use Cases Across Industries

Microsoft Azure has become a cornerstone for organizations looking to modernize their data infrastructure, gain actionable insights, and harness the power of AI and advanced analytics. From small startups to global enterprises, industries are embracing Azure's data services to address unique challenges, capitalize on emerging opportunities, and create smarter, data-driven ecosystems.

In this section, we explore how different sectors leverage Azure's data capabilities to drive innovation and efficiency. By examining real-world use cases across retail, healthcare, finance, manufacturing, government, and education, we'll understand how the platform's flexibility and breadth make it a universal solution for complex problems.

## Retail and E-commerce

The retail industry is undergoing a data-driven transformation, with Azure playing a vital role in enabling personalized experiences, real-time inventory tracking, and optimized supply chains.

### Use Case 1: Personalized Product Recommendations

Retailers use Azure Machine Learning and Azure Synapse Analytics to develop recommendation engines that provide tailored product suggestions to customers.

**Workflow:**

- **Data Ingestion:** Azure Data Factory collects clickstream data, purchase history, and demographic info.

- **Storage:** Azure Data Lake stores raw interaction logs and customer profiles.

- **Processing:** Azure Databricks is used to train collaborative filtering or content-based models.

- **Serving:** The model is deployed via Azure ML and integrated with e-commerce platforms.

**Code snippet: Sample pipeline for training a recommendation model using Azure ML**

```
from azureml.core import Workspace, Experiment

from azureml.train.automl import AutoMLConfig

from azureml.core.dataset import Dataset

ws = Workspace.from_config()

data = Dataset.Tabular.from_delimited_files(path="https://datalake/recommendation_data.csv")

automl_config = AutoMLConfig(

task='regression',

primary_metric='normalized_root_mean_squared_error',

training_data=data,

label_column_name='purchase_probability',
```

```
n_cross_validations=5,

compute_target='cpu-cluster'

)

experiment = Experiment(ws, 'product_recommendations')

run = experiment.submit(automl_config)
```

**Use Case 2: Real-Time Inventory and Fraud Detection**

Azure Stream Analytics, connected with Azure IoT Hub, enables real-time inventory monitoring. Retailers can also detect fraudulent activities at point-of-sale (POS) systems using anomaly detection models in real time.

Benefits:

- Avoid stockouts and overstocking.
- Detect suspicious transactions using Azure Cognitive Services.

---

## Healthcare

In healthcare, data is mission-critical. Azure provides the security, scalability, and compliance necessary to manage sensitive patient data, enable precision medicine, and modernize clinical workflows.

### Use Case 1: Electronic Health Record (EHR) Integration

Hospitals and clinics use Azure API Management and Azure Logic Apps to unify disparate EHR systems into a centralized, interoperable format.

**Workflow:**

- EHR systems publish data to Azure Event Hubs.
- Azure Functions normalize the schema.
- Data is stored in Azure SQL Database and analyzed in Azure Synapse.

### Use Case 2: Predictive Patient Care

Using historical patient records, lab results, and wearable device data, healthcare providers can build models to predict hospital readmissions, disease outbreaks, or ICU transfers.

**Azure Services Used:**

- Azure Data Lake for historical data storage.
- Azure ML for training predictive models.
- Power BI for clinician dashboards.
- Azure Purview for data governance and PII tracking.

**Security Consideration:** Azure offers services like Key Vault, Confidential Compute, and role-based access control to maintain HIPAA compliance.

## Financial Services

Financial institutions must process massive volumes of data with absolute reliability, transparency, and speed. Azure's robust suite of data services enables real-time risk analysis, fraud detection, and regulatory compliance.

### Use Case 1: Real-Time Fraud Detection

Banks use streaming data pipelines with Azure Event Hubs, Stream Analytics, and Azure ML to monitor for fraudulent activities across credit card transactions.

**Example:**

- A transaction with an unusual location and amount triggers a real-time scoring model.
- The model flags it for review.
- An automated logic app sends a notification to the fraud team.

### Use Case 2: Regulatory Reporting

With Azure Synapse Analytics and Azure Data Factory, financial institutions can automate and standardize regulatory reporting pipelines, ensuring transparency and auditability.

**Benefits:**

- Reduced manual intervention.
- Automated error detection and correction.

- Immutable audit trails using Azure Data Lake and Azure Immutable Blob Storage.

---

## Manufacturing

Manufacturers are leveraging Azure to implement smart factories, predictive maintenance, and energy optimization systems through the power of IoT and real-time analytics.

**Use Case 1: Predictive Maintenance**

IoT devices stream sensor data to Azure IoT Hub. Azure Machine Learning is used to predict potential equipment failures before they occur, reducing downtime and maintenance costs.

**Key Components:**

- IoT Hub for ingestion
- Azure Stream Analytics for real-time processing
- Azure Databricks for model training
- Power BI for technician dashboards

**Output Example:**

- Predictive maintenance model estimates the Remaining Useful Life (RUL) of a machine.
- Alerts are triggered when the RUL drops below a threshold.

### Use Case 2: Digital Twins for Factory Simulation

Using Azure Digital Twins, manufacturers create virtual representations of physical factories. They simulate workflow changes and optimize processes before implementing them physically.

**Advantages:**

- Reduce time-to-market for operational changes.
- Identify inefficiencies in layout, flow, or resource allocation.
- Integrate with Azure Maps for geospatial insights.

---

## Government and Public Sector

Governments require secure, transparent, and efficient data systems to manage services like public health, urban planning, and emergency response.

### Use Case 1: Smart City Infrastructure

Cities use Azure to aggregate data from traffic sensors, CCTV, and public transport systems. By analyzing data centrally in Azure Synapse, they can:

- Optimize traffic flow.
- Monitor air quality.
- Manage energy consumption.

**Example Setup:**

- Edge devices publish data to Azure IoT Edge.
- Data is sent to Azure Data Lake.
- Real-time dashboards inform decisions.

**Use Case 2: Citizen Services and Open Data**

With Azure Open Data Sets and Azure API Management, governments expose data to citizens, startups, and researchers, enabling innovation through transparency.

---

## Education and Research

Educational institutions and research bodies use Azure to create immersive learning experiences, enable scalable collaboration, and analyze research data at scale.

**Use Case 1: Personalized Learning Platforms**

Schools implement adaptive learning solutions powered by Azure ML that adjust coursework based on individual student performance.

Components:

- Azure SQL for storing student interactions.
- Azure Cognitive Services for sentiment analysis from student feedback.
- Power BI for teacher insights.

**Use Case 2: Genomic Research**

Using Azure Batch and Azure Blob Storage, research institutions can process massive genomic datasets in parallel.

**Workflow:**

- Raw data stored in Blob Storage.
- Parallel processing using Batch pools with custom containers.
- Results stored in Synapse for analysis.

---

## Cross-Industry Capabilities

Azure's versatility allows it to support universal use cases across industries:

- **Data Warehousing**: Synapse Analytics for scalable warehousing.
- **AI Enablement**: Azure ML and OpenAI for AI-driven services.
- **Serverless Architecture**: Azure Functions and Logic Apps to build cost-efficient, event-driven systems.
- **Data Governance**: Azure Purview ensures compliance with GDPR, HIPAA, and more.
- **Backup & Disaster Recovery**: Azure Backup, Site Recovery, and Immutable Blobs provide enterprise-grade protection.

## Final Thoughts

Azure's data services are designed to empower every industry to build intelligent, resilient, and scalable data solutions. By abstracting away infrastructure complexity and offering modular services, Azure allows developers, analysts, and architects to focus on value creation rather than system maintenance.

These real-world use cases illustrate how Azure is not just a toolset, but a transformative force. Whether optimizing retail operations, advancing patient care, detecting financial fraud, or enabling scientific breakthroughs, Azure provides the foundation for the next generation of data-driven innovation.

In the next chapter, we'll begin a hands-on journey through **Azure SQL Services**, starting with provisioning, managing, and securing relational data in the cloud.

# Chapter 2: Fundamentals of Azure SQL Services

## Introduction to Azure SQL Database

Azure SQL Database is Microsoft's flagship relational database-as-a-service (DBaaS), built on the mature SQL Server engine and designed to provide scalable, highly available, and secure SQL capabilities in the cloud. It is a fully managed platform-as-a-service (PaaS) offering that handles many of the administrative burdens traditionally associated with SQL Server such as backups, patching, scaling, and high availability, freeing developers and DBAs to focus on application performance and business logic.

This section explores what Azure SQL Database is, why it's important, and how it fits within the wider Azure data ecosystem. We will also break down the different deployment models, core features, and the reasons organizations are choosing it over traditional on-premise databases.

---

### What is Azure SQL Database?

Azure SQL Database is a cloud-based relational database that supports T-SQL (Transact-SQL) queries and provides full compatibility with the core features of SQL Server. It is designed for high availability and optimized performance, and offers flexible pricing and scalability models suitable for applications of all sizes.

Key characteristics:

- Fully managed: Microsoft handles infrastructure management, high availability, backups, and patches.

- Built-in intelligence: Performance tuning and threat detection.
- Elastic: Instantly scale up/down or out/in to meet demand.
- Secure: Role-based access, encryption, and auditing built-in.

Azure SQL Database runs on the latest stable version of the SQL Server engine and is regularly updated. It supports modern development practices and tools, including CI/CD pipelines, GitHub integration, and RESTful APIs.

---

## Deployment Models

Azure SQL Database provides several deployment options to accommodate different workloads and organizational needs:

### 1. Single Database

This is a fully isolated database optimized for modern cloud applications. Ideal for microservices or multi-tenant applications where each customer gets their own database.

Features:

- Independent compute and storage.
- Simple cost management.
- Autoscaling based on DTUs or vCores.

Example Use Case: SaaS platform allocating a database per customer.

**2. Elastic Pool**

An elastic pool allows multiple databases to share a pool of resources, which is more cost-effective for variable or unpredictable workloads.

Benefits:

- Shared vCores or DTUs among databases.
- Automatically distributes resources where needed.
- Lower total cost of ownership.

Example Use Case: A portfolio of small applications with sporadic usage patterns.

**3. Managed Instance**

Azure SQL Managed Instance is closest to a lift-and-shift for on-prem SQL Server. It offers nearly 100% compatibility with on-premise features including SQL Agent, Service Broker, CLR, and more.

Key Capabilities:

- Support for cross-database queries.
- Native VNET support.
- Ideal for legacy workloads and hybrid architectures.

Example Use Case: Migrating an enterprise ERP or CRM from on-prem to Azure.

## Core Features and Capabilities

### 1. High Availability

Azure SQL Database guarantees 99.99% uptime through features like:

- Zone redundant deployments.
- Automatic failover using availability zones.
- Transparent geo-replication with up to four readable secondaries.

### 2. Automated Backups and Restore

Azure SQL automatically performs:

- Full backups every week.
- Differential backups every 12 hours.
- Transaction log backups every 5–10 minutes.

Point-in-time restore is supported for up to 35 days depending on tier.

Example CLI command to restore a database:

```
az sql db restore \
—dest-name RestoredDB \
—name OriginalDB \
—resource-group MyGroup \
```

—server MyServer \

—time "2025-03-01T13:00:00Z"

**3. Scalability**

Two primary purchasing models:

- **DTU-based**: Combines CPU, memory, and IOPS into a single bundle.
- **vCore-based**: Separates compute and storage for more flexibility.

Scalability is horizontal (elastic pools) or vertical (change service tier), and can be done manually or automatically via APIs or CLI.

**4. Intelligent Performance**

Built-in performance tuning capabilities:

- **Query Performance Insight**: Visualize top resource-consuming queries.
- **Automatic Index Management**: SQL Database can automatically create/drop indexes based on usage.
- **Query Store**: Historical tracking of query plans and performance.

Example: Enabling automatic tuning

az sql db automatic-tuning update \

—name mydb \

—server myserver \

—resource-group mygroup \

—desired-state Auto

## Security in Azure SQL Database

Security is a major priority in the cloud. Azure SQL includes advanced protection mechanisms to ensure data integrity and compliance.

### 1. Authentication and Authorization

- **Azure Active Directory (AAD)** integration for centralized identity management.
- **SQL Authentication** using usernames and passwords.
- Role-Based Access Control (RBAC) for fine-grained permission management.

### 2. Encryption

- **Transparent Data Encryption (TDE)**: Encrypts data at rest.
- **Always Encrypted**: Protects sensitive data even from DBAs.
- **SSL/TLS**: Encrypts data in transit.

**3. Auditing and Threat Detection**

- Built-in auditing logs events and writes them to storage.
- Threat Detection notifies of suspicious activity like SQL injection or anomalous access.

Example to enable auditing:

```
az sql db audit-policy update \
—name mydb \
—server myserver \
—resource-group mygroup \
—state Enabled \
—storage-account myauditstorage
```

---

## Integration with Developer and DevOps Workflows

Azure SQL Database integrates with modern development and CI/CD pipelines:

- Support for **GitHub Actions** and **Azure DevOps Pipelines**.
- **ARM templates**, **Terraform**, and **Bicep** for infrastructure automation.
- Integration with **Visual Studio, VS Code, SSMS**, and **Azure Data Studio**.

Example: Deploying Azure SQL with Terraform

```
resource "azurerm_sql_server" "example" {
name = "sqlserverdemo"
resource_group_name = azurerm_resource_group.example.name
location = azurerm_resource_group.example.location
version = "12.0"
administrator_login = "adminuser"
administrator_login_password = "StrongPassword123!"
}
resource "azurerm_sql_database" "example" {
name = "exampledb"
resource_group_name = azurerm_resource_group.example.name
location = azurerm_sql_server.example.location
server_name = azurerm_sql_server.example.name
sku_name = "S0"
}
```

## Business Continuity and Disaster Recovery (BCDR)

Azure SQL provides built-in BCDR features:

- **Geo-replication**: Configures readable secondaries in different regions.

- **Auto-failover groups**: Automate failover for multiple databases.
- **Long-term retention**: Archive backups for up to 10 years.

These features are critical for mission-critical applications that require uninterrupted service.

---

## Common Use Cases

### Web Applications

Ideal for backend storage for web apps built on .NET, Node.js, Java, or Python. Integration with Azure App Service provides auto-scaling and global availability.

### SaaS Applications

Multi-tenant SaaS platforms use elastic pools to manage thousands of tenant databases efficiently.

### Analytics and Reporting

Data can be ingested into Azure SQL from operational systems and then queried directly or exported into Azure Synapse for analytical processing.

### Hybrid Deployments

With support for Azure Arc and Managed Instance, SQL workloads can run in hybrid scenarios where compliance or latency requires on-premise components.

### Summary

Azure SQL Database represents the evolution of relational data services in the cloud. It combines the robustness of SQL Server with the flexibility and scalability of Azure. By eliminating infrastructure management and integrating with modern tools and services, it enables teams to deliver applications faster, more securely, and with greater agility.

Whether you're building a microservice, migrating legacy systems, or architecting a data platform from scratch, Azure SQL Database is a foundational service in your cloud toolkit. In the following sections, we'll explore how to provision and configure SQL databases, manage and query data, and optimize for performance and cost.

## Provisioning and Configuring SQL Databases

Provisioning and configuring Azure SQL Databases is one of the foundational tasks for any data solution in the cloud. Azure provides multiple tools and interfaces—portal, CLI, PowerShell, ARM templates, Bicep, and Terraform—to create and configure databases efficiently. This section offers a comprehensive, step-by-step guide on setting up SQL databases in Azure, configuring networking and access controls, selecting service tiers, and tuning resources for performance and cost optimization.

### Creating an Azure SQL Database

The first step is provisioning a SQL server and then creating a database within that server. This can be done via the Azure Portal for a graphical interface or programmatically using the CLI or Terraform.

**Via Azure CLI**

```
# Login to Azure

az login

# Create a resource group

az group create—name sql-rg—location eastus

# Create a logical SQL server

az sql server create \

—name my-sql-server-001 \

—resource-group sql-rg \

—location eastus \

—admin-user sqladmin \

—admin-password StrongP@ssw0rd!

# Create a database

az sql db create \

—resource-group sql-rg \

—server my-sql-server-001 \

—name mydatabase \

—service-objective S0
```

This script creates a basic SQL server and a single S0-tier database with minimal cost, suitable for development or small-scale applications.

## Choosing a Service Tier

Azure SQL offers different pricing and performance models to match various workload types.

### DTU-Based Model

- Combines CPU, memory, and IO.
- Suitable for predictable workloads.
- Tiers: Basic, Standard (S0-S12), Premium (P1-P15).

### vCore-Based Model

- Separates compute and storage.
- Ideal for scaling and cost visibility.
- Offers General Purpose, Business Critical, and Hyperscale tiers.

| Model | Best For | Scaling | SLA |
|---|---|---|---|
| DTU | Simple, predictable workloads | Manual | 99.99% |
| vCore | High-performance workloads | Manual/ Auto | 99.99%-99.995% |
| Hyperscale | Massive OLTP databases | Auto scale | 99.99% |

### Selecting Compute Tier Example via CLI

az sql db create \

—name prod-db \

```
—resource-group sql-rg \
—server my-sql-server-001 \
—edition GeneralPurpose \
—compute-model Provisioned \
—family Gen5 \
—capacity 4 \
—max-size 10GB
```

## Configuring Networking and Access

Azure SQL databases are protected by default, allowing access only from specific IP ranges or private endpoints.

### Setting a Firewall Rule

To allow client access from a known IP range:

```
az sql server firewall-rule create \
—resource-group sql-rg \
—server my-sql-server-001 \
—name AllowMyIP \
—start-ip-address 203.0.113.5 \
—end-ip-address 203.0.113.5
```

### Enabling Private Endpoint Access

For secure access over Azure Virtual Networks (VNets):

1. Enable VNet service endpoint or private endpoint.
2. Use Azure DNS or custom DNS integration.

### Enforcing TLS Encryption

TLS encryption is mandatory for Azure SQL to secure data in transit. No additional configuration is typically needed, but client libraries must support it.

---

## Authentication and Authorization

Azure SQL supports two primary authentication methods:

### SQL Authentication

- Traditional username and password.
- Ideal for applications or users outside Azure AD.

### Azure Active Directory Authentication

- Uses Azure AD identities.
- Centralized credential management.
- Enables conditional access policies.

Example: Adding an Azure AD Admin

```
az sql server ad-admin create \
```

```
—resource-group sql-rg \

—server my-sql-server-001 \

—display-name "Contoso Admin" \

—object-id <AzureAD_Object_ID>
```

## Configuring Geo-Replication and Backups

### Enabling Geo-Replication

Azure SQL supports active geo-replication, allowing up to four readable secondary replicas in different Azure regions.

```
az sql db replica create \

—name mydatabase \

—resource-group sql-rg \

—server my-sql-server-001 \

—partner-server secondary-sql-server \

—partner-resource-group sql-rg
```

### Backup and Restore

Backups are automated:

- Full backups every week.
- Differential backups every 12 hours.
- Transaction log backups every 5-10 minutes.

Restore to any point in the retention period.

## Advanced Configuration Options

### Transparent Data Encryption (TDE)

Enabled by default for all new databases. Protects data at rest.

az sql db tde set \

—status Enabled \

—database mydatabase \

—server my-sql-server-001 \

—resource-group sql-rg

### Auditing

Write audit logs to a storage account or Log Analytics.

az sql db audit-policy update \

—name mydatabase \

—server my-sql-server-001 \

—resource-group sql-rg \

—state Enabled \

—storage-account myauditstorage

**Threat Detection**

Proactively detects suspicious activities like brute force login attempts or SQL injection.

## Using ARM Templates and Terraform for Declarative Provisioning

For automated and repeatable deployments, infrastructure as code is essential.

**ARM Template Snippet**

```
{
"type": "Microsoft.Sql/servers/databases",
"name": "[concat(parameters('sqlServerName'), '/', parameters('databaseName'))]",
"apiVersion": "2022-02-01-preview",
"location": "[parameters('location')]",
"properties": {
"collation": "SQL_Latin1_General_CP1_CI_AS",
"maxSizeBytes": "2147483648",
"sampleName": "AdventureWorksLT"
},
"sku": {
"name": "S0",
```

```
"tier": "Standard",
"capacity": 10
}
}
```

**Terraform Snippet**

```
resource "azurerm_sql_database" "main" {
name = "main-db"
resource_group_name = azurerm_resource_group.main.name
location = azurerm_sql_server.main.location
server_name = azurerm_sql_server.main.name
sku_name = "S0"
}
```

---

## Performance Configuration Best Practices

- Use **Query Store** to track and compare execution plans.
- Enable **automatic tuning** for index management.
- Allocate IOPS and CPU based on expected query loads.
- Partition large tables where needed.
- Regularly review DTU/vCore usage and adjust tiers.

---

## Monitoring and Diagnostics

Monitoring tools available:

- **Azure Monitor**: Platform-level metrics.
- **Log Analytics**: Custom query support with Kusto Query Language (KQL).
- **SQL Insights**: Deep integration with SQL Server metrics.

Example: Querying CPU utilization

```
AzureMetrics
| where Resource == "mydatabase"
| where MetricName == "cpu_percent"
| summarize avg(Total) by bin(TimeGenerated, 1h)
```

## Summary

Provisioning and configuring Azure SQL Databases is a flexible and scalable process that can be performed using various tools tailored to both beginners and seasoned DevOps professionals. Whether you're deploying a development environment or configuring a globally redundant enterprise database, Azure SQL gives you the necessary tools to manage the entire lifecycle effectively—from creation and access control to performance tuning and disaster recovery.

Understanding and mastering this foundational step ensures a solid base for future development, analytics, and integration efforts within Azure's data ecosystem. In the next section, we'll dive into querying and managing data in Azure SQL, including CRUD operations, advanced joins, and performance techniques for efficient querying at scale.

## Querying and Managing Data

Once an Azure SQL Database has been provisioned and configured, the next critical step is working with the data it holds. Querying and managing data in Azure SQL follows many of the same principles as traditional SQL Server environments but is enriched with cloud-native capabilities such as intelligent performance tuning, advanced security features, and powerful monitoring tools.

In this section, we'll explore how to create and manage schemas, insert and manipulate data, write effective queries, use views and stored procedures, apply indexing strategies, handle data integrity, and utilize Azure-specific management tools for maintaining operational excellence.

### Schema Design and Table Creation

A solid schema design is the backbone of performance and maintainability. Tables should be normalized where appropriate, keys must be thoughtfully defined, and naming conventions should be consistent.

**Creating Tables**

```
CREATE TABLE Customers (

CustomerID INT PRIMARY KEY IDENTITY(1,1),

FirstName NVARCHAR(50),

LastName NVARCHAR(50),
```

Email NVARCHAR(100) UNIQUE,

DateJoined DATETIME2 DEFAULT GETDATE()

);

**Creating Related Tables**

CREATE TABLE Orders (

OrderID INT PRIMARY KEY IDENTITY(1,1),

CustomerID INT FOREIGN KEY REFERENCES Customers(CustomerID),

OrderDate DATETIME2 DEFAULT GETDATE(),

TotalAmount DECIMAL(10, 2)

);

## Basic Data Operations

CRUD operations (Create, Read, Update, Delete) are essential to managing relational data.

**Insert Data**

INSERT INTO Customers (FirstName, LastName, Email)

VALUES ('John', 'Doe', 'john.doe@example.com');

**Read Data**

SELECT FirstName, LastName, Email

```
FROM Customers

WHERE DateJoined > '2024-01-01';
```

**Update Data**

```
UPDATE Customers

SET Email = 'john.new@example.com'

WHERE CustomerID = 1;
```

**Delete Data**

```
DELETE FROM Customers

WHERE CustomerID = 1;
```

---

## Advanced Querying

To gain powerful insights from data, you must go beyond basic SELECT statements.

**Joins**

```
SELECT c.FirstName, c.LastName, o.OrderDate, o.TotalAmount

FROM Customers c

JOIN Orders o ON c.CustomerID = o.CustomerID

WHERE o.OrderDate BETWEEN '2024-01-01' AND '2024-12-31';
```

**Subqueries and CTEs**

```
—Using a Common Table Expression (CTE)

WITH TopCustomers AS (

SELECT CustomerID, COUNT(*) AS OrdersCount

FROM Orders

GROUP BY CustomerID

HAVING COUNT(*) > 5

)

SELECT c.FirstName, c.LastName, t.OrdersCount

FROM TopCustomers t

JOIN Customers c ON t.CustomerID = c.CustomerID;
```

**Aggregations**

```
SELECT CustomerID, SUM(TotalAmount) AS TotalSpent

FROM Orders

GROUP BY CustomerID

ORDER BY TotalSpent DESC;
```

## Views, Stored Procedures, and Functions

These constructs promote code reuse, encapsulation, and security.

**Views**

```
CREATE VIEW ActiveCustomers AS

SELECT CustomerID, FirstName, LastName

FROM Customers

WHERE DateJoined > DATEADD(year, -1, GETDATE());
```

**Stored Procedures**

```
CREATE PROCEDURE GetCustomerOrders

@CustomerID INT

AS

BEGIN

SELECT * FROM Orders

WHERE CustomerID = @CustomerID;

END;
```

**Scalar Functions**

```
CREATE FUNCTION GetFullName (@FirstName NVARCHAR(50), @LastName NVARCHAR(50))

RETURNS NVARCHAR(101)

AS

BEGIN
```

```
RETURN CONCAT(@FirstName, ' ', @LastName);
END;
```

## Indexing and Performance Optimization

Indexes are critical for performance, especially on large datasets. However, they must be used wisely to avoid excessive maintenance overhead.

### Creating Indexes

```
CREATE INDEX IX_Orders_CustomerID ON Orders(CustomerID);
```

### Using Execution Plans

Azure Data Studio and SSMS provide visual query plans to analyze performance bottlenecks like:

- Table scans
- Missing indexes
- Expensive joins

### Index Fragmentation

Monitor and rebuild indexes periodically:

```
ALTER INDEX ALL ON Orders
REBUILD;
```

Or use automated maintenance tasks with Azure Automation or Elastic Jobs.

---

## Data Integrity and Constraints

Maintaining high data quality requires constraints and validation mechanisms.

### Constraints

- Primary keys
- Foreign keys
- Unique constraints
- Default values
- Check constraints

Example:

ALTER TABLE Orders

ADD CONSTRAINT CK_TotalAmount_Positive CHECK (TotalAmount > 0);

### Transactions

Use transactions to ensure atomicity:

BEGIN TRANSACTION;

UPDATE Customers SET Email = 'jane@example.com' WHERE CustomerID = 2;

INSERT INTO Orders (CustomerID, TotalAmount) VALUES (2, 150.00);

COMMIT TRANSACTION;

Use ROLLBACK for error scenarios.

---

## Temporal Tables and Auditing

Temporal tables track changes to data over time automatically.

**Create a Temporal Table**

CREATE TABLE Products (

ProductID INT PRIMARY KEY,

ProductName NVARCHAR(100),

Price DECIMAL(10,2),

ValidFrom DATETIME2 GENERATED ALWAYS AS ROW START,

ValidTo DATETIME2 GENERATED ALWAYS AS ROW END,

PERIOD FOR SYSTEM_TIME (ValidFrom, ValidTo)

)

WITH (SYSTEM_VERSIONING = ON);

**Query Historical Data**

SELECT * FROM Products

FOR SYSTEM_TIME BETWEEN '2024-01-01' AND '2024-06-01';

## Security at the Data Level

### Row-Level Security

Enforce access control by filtering rows based on user identity.

```
CREATE FUNCTION dbo.fn_securitypredicate(@UserID INT)
RETURNS TABLE
WITH SCHEMABINDING
AS
RETURN SELECT 1 AS fn_securitypredicate_result
WHERE @UserID = CAST(SESSION_CONTEXT(N'UserID') AS INT);
CREATE SECURITY POLICY OrderFilter
ADD FILTER PREDICATE dbo.fn_securitypredicate(CustomerID)
ON Orders
WITH (STATE = ON);
```

Set user context in the session:

```
EXEC sp_set_session_context 'UserID', 5;
```

## Managing and Monitoring Data

### Azure SQL Insights

Enables granular monitoring via Azure Monitor.

### Query Performance Insight

Highlights:

- Top CPU-consuming queries
- Query duration trends
- Recommendations for indexing

### Using KQL for Analysis in Log Analytics

```
AzureDiagnostics
| where Resource == "mydatabase"
| where OperationName == "ExecuteQuery"
| summarize avg(DurationMs) by bin(TimeGenerated, 1h), StatementType
```

---

## Tools for Data Management

- **Azure Data Studio**: Cross-platform with built-in notebooks.
- **SQL Server Management Studio (SSMS)**: Full-featured admin and query tool.

- **Azure Portal**: Basic data exploration and quick edits.
- **Azure CLI & PowerShell**: Scripting and automation for routine tasks.

---

## Automation and Scripting

Use T-SQL scripts or CLI commands for scheduled jobs, backups, or batch inserts. Elastic Jobs can execute these across multiple databases.

Example: Scheduled data purge

```
DELETE FROM Logs

WHERE LogDate < DATEADD(month, -3, GETDATE());
```

---

## Summary

Efficiently querying and managing data is the essence of working with Azure SQL Database. From schema design and CRUD operations to advanced query tuning, temporal tables, and automation, Azure SQL provides a rich, SQL Server-compatible environment with added benefits of scalability, integrated security, and cloud intelligence.

Organizations can start small and grow their systems seamlessly, with tools and features that cater to both traditional relational database use cases and modern cloud-first workloads. In the next section, we'll focus specifically on tuning database performance and optimizing cost across different workloads and configurations.

# Performance Tuning and Cost Optimization

Maximizing performance while minimizing cost is one of the primary goals of any data solution architecting with Azure SQL Database. As a cloud-native platform, Azure SQL offers a rich set of tools and configurations that allow developers, database administrators, and data engineers to tune workloads, automate performance improvements, and optimize expenditure based on demand.

This section provides a detailed exploration of best practices and strategies for tuning SQL performance, identifying bottlenecks, scaling resources, optimizing query execution, and leveraging built-in automation to reduce cost without sacrificing throughput or reliability.

---

## Understanding Performance Metrics

Before tuning, it's essential to understand which performance indicators are critical for evaluating the health and efficiency of your SQL database.

**Core Metrics:**

- **CPU utilization** – Measures how much processing power is consumed.
- **DTU or vCore usage** – Indicates the percentage of resource consumption.
- **IO latency** – Speed at which data is read/written to storage.
- **Query duration** – Time taken for execution.

- **Blocking and deadlocks** – Signs of contention in transactions.

These metrics can be collected using:

- **Azure Monitor**
- **Query Performance Insight**
- **Dynamic Management Views (DMVs)**
- **SQL Insights (preview)**

**Sample DMV Query:**

```
SELECT TOP 10

qs.total_elapsed_time / qs.execution_count AS AvgElapsedTime,

qs.execution_count,

qs.total_logical_reads,

qs.total_worker_time,

SUBSTRING(qt.text, qs.statement_start_offset / 2,

(CASE WHEN qs.statement_end_offset = -1

THEN LEN(CONVERT(NVARCHAR(MAX), qt.text)) * 2

ELSE qs.statement_end_offset END - qs.statement_start_offset) / 2) AS query_text

FROM sys.dm_exec_query_stats AS qs

CROSS APPLY sys.dm_exec_sql_text(qs.sql_handle) AS qt
```

ORDER BY AvgElapsedTime DESC;

## Automatic Tuning

Azure SQL Database comes with built-in intelligence that continuously analyzes query performance and provides tuning recommendations or automatically implements them.

**Capabilities:**

- **Automatic Index Management** – Adds or drops indexes based on usage patterns.
- **Force Last Known Good Plan** – Prevents performance regression due to bad query plans.

**Enabling Auto-Tuning:**

```
az sql db automatic-tuning update \
—name mydatabase \
—server myserver \
—resource-group mygroup \
—desired-state Auto
```

You can also enable individual tuning actions:

- createIndex
- dropIndex
- forceLastGoodPlan

**View Recommendations:**

```
SELECT * FROM sys.database_automatic_tuning;
```

## Index Optimization

Indexes improve query performance but come at a cost: increased storage usage and write overhead. A well-optimized index strategy balances performance with maintainability.

**Best Practices:**

- Use **clustered indexes** on primary key columns.
- Create **non-clustered indexes** on frequently filtered or joined columns.
- Use **included columns** for covering indexes.
- Avoid over-indexing: each insert/update/delete incurs index maintenance.

**Fragmentation Check:**

```
SELECT
dbschemas.[name] AS 'Schema',
dbtables.[name] AS 'Table',
dbindexes.[name] AS 'Index',
indexstats.avg_fragmentation_in_percent
```

FROM sys.dm_db_index_physical_stats (DB_ID(), NULL, NULL, NULL, 'LIMITED') indexstats

JOIN sys.tables dbtables ON dbtables.[object_id] = indexstats.[object_id]

JOIN sys.schemas dbschemas ON dbtables.[schema_id] = dbschemas.[schema_id]

JOIN sys.indexes AS dbindexes ON dbindexes.[object_id] = indexstats.[object_id]

AND indexstats.index_id = dbindexes.index_id

WHERE indexstats.avg_fragmentation_in_percent > 20;

**Rebuild or Reorganize:**

ALTER INDEX [IX_Orders_CustomerID] ON Orders

REBUILD;

Or automate via scheduled jobs using **Elastic Job Agent** or **Azure Automation.**

---

## Query Optimization

Even with the best hardware, poorly written queries can ruin performance. Key optimization strategies include:

1. **Avoid SELECT ***

Use explicit column names to reduce memory usage and IO.

—Inefficient

SELECT * FROM Customers;

—Optimized

SELECT FirstName, LastName, Email FROM Customers;

**2. Parameterization**

Prevents query plan cache bloat and improves execution time.

—Good

SELECT * FROM Orders WHERE CustomerID = @CustomerID;

—Bad

SELECT * FROM Orders WHERE CustomerID = 1234;

**3. Query Store**

Tracks performance of queries over time and retains historical execution plans.

Enable Query Store:

ALTER DATABASE [mydatabase]

SET QUERY_STORE = ON;

Use Query Store views to identify regressions:

SELECT

qsqt.query_sql_text,

qsp.execution_type_desc,

qsp.avg_duration,

qsp.count_executions

FROM sys.query_store_plan AS qsp

JOIN sys.query_store_query AS qsq ON qsp.query_id = qsq.query_id

JOIN sys.query_store_query_text AS qsqt ON qsq.query_text_id = qsqt.query_text_id

WHERE qsp.avg_duration > 1000;

---

## Elastic Pool Optimization

When using elastic pools, you must ensure resource sharing does not lead to contention or underutilization.

### Monitor Resource Utilization

- Analyze database-level usage metrics.
- Use **DTU per second** graphs to determine peak loads.
- Implement **scale-up/scale-down automation** during business hours.

### Cost Strategy:

- Place highly variable usage databases in pools.
- Place heavy, stable-load databases on single instances.

---

## Cost Optimization Strategies

Azure provides pricing flexibility through compute and storage decoupling (vCore model), auto-scaling, and reserved capacity discounts.

### 1. Reserved Instances

Purchase 1-year or 3-year reservations for significant discounts.

az sql db show \

—name mydatabase \

—resource-group mygroup \

—server myserver \

—query "sku"

Use this output to determine eligibility for reserved pricing.

### 2. Auto-Pause and Auto-Resume

Use **serverless** tier for intermittent workloads:

- Automatically pauses after inactivity.
- Automatically resumes on activity.

az sql db create \

—name serverless-db \

—server myserver \

—resource-group mygroup \

—edition GeneralPurpose \

—compute-model Serverless \

—auto-pause-delay 60 \

—min-capacity 0.5 \

—max-capacity 4

**3. Storage Tiering**

Use **Geo-Redundant Storage (GRS)** only for mission-critical scenarios. Use **Locally Redundant Storage (LRS)** for development/test environments to reduce cost.

---

## Monitoring Tools

Azure offers several tools for proactive and reactive monitoring:

**Azure Monitor**

- Visualizes key metrics.
- Sets up alerts for high CPU, deadlocks, or failed connections.

**Log Analytics**

- Query logs with KQL.
- Create dashboards for daily/weekly trends.

Sample KQL:

```
AzureDiagnostics
| where ResourceType == "DATABASES"
| where OperationName == "ExecuteQuery"
| summarize AvgDuration = avg(DurationMs) by bin(TimeGenerated, 1h)
```

### Alerts and Budgeting

Set budgets and alerts to avoid overspending:

```
az consumption budget create \
—amount 100 \
—category cost \
—name "monthly-sql-budget" \
—resource-group mygroup \
—time-grain Monthly \
—time-period start=2025-01-01T00:00:00Z end=2025-12-31T00:00:00Z
```

## Scaling Best Practices

### Vertical Scaling

- Increase vCores or DTUs to handle predictable workload spikes.

- Monitor for diminishing returns; higher tiers may yield marginal gains.

**Horizontal Scaling**

- Use **read replicas** for scaling SELECT-heavy workloads.
- Use **Elastic Jobs** to batch-write data across shards.
- Consider **Synapse Link** for analytics workloads without hitting OLTP systems.

---

## Summary

Performance tuning and cost optimization in Azure SQL Database is a continuous and dynamic process. It requires a combination of intelligent tooling, strategic indexing, efficient query writing, and thoughtful tier selection. Leveraging built-in features such as automatic tuning, Query Store, and serverless compute ensures that workloads run efficiently while keeping costs predictable and manageable.

By aligning workload patterns with appropriate service tiers, automating resource management, and consistently monitoring query behavior, organizations can achieve high-performance data platforms that scale effortlessly and remain financially sustainable.

The next section will explore security and compliance considerations—an equally critical dimension of operating in the cloud. From encryption and role-based access to auditing and advanced threat protection, you'll learn how Azure SQL Database helps you meet internal and regulatory standards.

# Security and Compliance Considerations

Security and compliance are non-negotiable components of any enterprise-grade database solution. In the cloud, these responsibilities are shared between the cloud provider and the customer. Azure SQL Database, a platform-as-a-service (PaaS) offering, delivers a comprehensive set of built-in security features and compliance controls to help you safeguard sensitive data, control access, detect threats, and meet regulatory requirements across industries.

This section dives into the extensive security architecture of Azure SQL Database, including authentication and authorization mechanisms, encryption models, network security options, auditing and monitoring capabilities, advanced threat protection, and compliance alignment.

---

## The Shared Responsibility Model

Understanding the **shared responsibility model** is key to proper cloud security posture:

| Responsibility Area | Microsoft (Azure) | Customer |
|---|---|---|
| Physical datacenter security | � | � |
| Hardware and host OS | � | � |
| SQL Database software patches | � | � |
| Identity and access management | � | � |
| Data classification and labeling | � | � |
| Application security | � | � |
| Auditing and compliance policy | � | � |

You are responsible for securing **data**, **identities**, and **access controls**. Azure takes care of physical security, infrastructure, and platform integrity.

---

## Authentication Methods

### 1. SQL Authentication

- Username/password based.
- Used by applications and legacy systems.

CREATE LOGIN AppUser WITH PASSWORD = 'StrongP@ss123!';

CREATE USER AppUser FOR LOGIN AppUser;

ALTER ROLE db_datareader ADD MEMBER AppUser;

**Best practices:**

- Use complex passwords.
- Rotate credentials periodically.
- Store credentials securely (e.g., Azure Key Vault).

### 2. Azure Active Directory (AAD) Authentication

- Integrates with enterprise identity systems.
- Enables single sign-on (SSO).
- Supports multi-factor authentication (MFA).

az sql server ad-admin create \

—resource-group mygroup \

—server myserver \

—display-name "Contoso Admin" \

—object-id <aad-user-object-id>

Use AAD groups for RBAC:

CREATE USER [aadgroup@contoso.com] FROM EXTERNAL PROVIDER;

ALTER ROLE db_owner ADD MEMBER [aadgroup@contoso.com];

## Authorization and Role Management

Azure SQL supports role-based access control using fixed and custom roles.

**Built-in Database Roles:**

- db_owner: Full access to all DB resources.
- db_datareader: Read-only access.
- db_datawriter: Write access.
- db_ddladmin: Schema modifications.

Assigning a role:

ALTER ROLE db_datareader ADD MEMBER AppUser;

Use **separation of duties** to restrict admin vs. application access. Never use a single account for all operations.

## Encryption Capabilities

Azure SQL provides end-to-end encryption capabilities covering data at rest, in transit, and in use.

**1. Transparent Data Encryption (TDE)**

- Enabled by default.
- Encrypts database, log, and backup files.
- Uses built-in or customer-managed keys (CMK) via Azure Key Vault.

```
az sql db tde set \
—name mydatabase \
—server myserver \
—resource-group mygroup \
—status Enabled
```

**2. Always Encrypted**

- Protects sensitive columns (e.g., SSNs, card numbers).
- Encryption keys are held client-side.
- Prevents access by DBAs or Azure staff.

```
CREATE COLUMN MASTER KEY CMK1
WITH (
```

```
KEY_STORE_PROVIDER_NAME = 'AZURE_KEY_VAULT',
KEY_PATH = 'https://myvault.vault.azure.net/keys/cmkey/'
);
CREATE COLUMN ENCRYPTION KEY CEK1
WITH VALUES (
COLUMN_MASTER_KEY = CMK1,
ALGORITHM = 'RSA_OAEP',
ENCRYPTED_VALUE = 0x...
);
```

**3. SSL/TLS Encryption**

- Required for all Azure SQL connections.
- Enforced via connection strings or server settings.

---

## Network Security

Protecting access to Azure SQL is crucial to prevent unauthorized data exposure.

**1. Firewall Rules**

Restrict access to trusted IP addresses.

```
az sql server firewall-rule create \
—resource-group mygroup \
```

—server myserver \

—name AllowHome \

—start-ip-address 203.0.113.10 \

—end-ip-address 203.0.113.10

**2. Private Link**

- Allows secure access over Azure VNet.
- Bypasses public internet.
- Provides isolation for highly sensitive workloads.

az network private-endpoint create \

—name sql-private-endpoint \

—resource-group mygroup \

—vnet-name my-vnet \

—subnet my-subnet \

—private-connection-resource-id <SQL_SERVER_RESOURCE_ID> \

—group-ids sqlServer

**3. Virtual Network Service Endpoints**

Provides optimized routing and access control using VNet rules.

## Auditing and Logging

Auditing is key for both operational and compliance monitoring.

**Enabling Auditing:**

az sql db audit-policy update \

—name mydatabase \

—server myserver \

—resource-group mygroup \

—state Enabled \

—storage-account myauditstorage

**Outputs:**

- Storage Account
- Log Analytics Workspace
- Event Hub (optional)

**Use Cases:**

- Track who accessed what and when.
- Detect unauthorized modifications.
- Produce audit trails for compliance (HIPAA, SOC, GDPR).

---

## Advanced Threat Protection

Azure SQL Advanced Data Security provides intelligent, real-time threat detection and vulnerability scanning.

**Components:**

1. **Vulnerability Assessment**

   ○ Identifies misconfigurations.

   ○ Assesses compliance against best practices.

2. **Threat Detection**

   ○ Alerts on SQL injection, brute-force attacks, anomalous access.

**Enabling Threat Detection:**

```
az sql db threat-policy update \
—name mydatabase \
—server myserver \
—resource-group mygroup \
—state Enabled \
—email-addresses admin@contoso.com
```

Alerts are integrated with Azure Defender and can trigger Logic Apps for automated remediation.

## Data Classification and Labeling

Azure SQL Database supports automatic data classification to help you:

- Identify sensitive data.
- Apply labels (Confidential, Restricted).
- Prioritize security policies.

Enable via the Azure Portal or SQL:

```
ADD SENSITIVITY CLASSIFICATION TO
dbo.Customers.Email
WITH (LABEL='Confidential', INFORMATION_TYPE='Contact Info', RANK=High);
```

Reports can be exported for compliance audits.

---

## Compliance Certifications

Azure SQL Database is certified for over 100 standards globally, including:

| Standard | Industry | Region |
|---|---|---|
| HIPAA | Healthcare | US |
| ISO/IEC 27001 | General security | Global |
| SOC 1, 2, 3 | Financial/IT Ops | US/Global |
| PCI DSS | Payments | Global |
| GDPR | Data privacy | EU |
| FedRAMP | Government | US |

Use Azure's **Compliance Manager** to assess risk, assign controls, and track progress toward certifications.

## Monitoring Security with Azure Defender

Azure Defender for SQL provides:

- **Advanced Threat Protection** (included)
- **Vulnerability scans**
- **Integration with Microsoft Sentinel** (SIEM)

Alerts can be visualized in Azure Security Center and used to automate incident responses.

Example KQL for Sentinel:

```
SecurityAlert
| where ProductName == "Azure SQL Database"
| where AlertName contains "SQL Injection"
| summarize count() by bin(TimeGenerated, 1h), Resource
```

## Key Vault Integration

Storing keys, passwords, and certificates in Azure Key Vault helps centralize secrets management.

**Access from SQL:**

- Used for TDE with customer-managed keys (CMK).
- Required for Always Encrypted.

Example: Granting SQL Server access to Key Vault

```
az keyvault set-policy \
—name myvault \
—object-id <sql-server-principal-id> \
—key-permissions get unwrapKey wrapKey
```

## Summary

Azure SQL Database provides a powerful suite of tools to ensure that your data is protected, your access is controlled, and your environment is compliant with both internal and external standards. From the moment a database is provisioned, features like encryption, access control, auditing, and threat protection are either automatically enabled or easily configurable.

Security in Azure SQL is not a single checkbox—it's a layered defense strategy supported by intelligent services and rigorous global compliance. Whether you're building a regulated healthcare application or simply securing an internal reporting tool, Azure SQL gives you the framework to meet security goals without compromise.

In the next chapter, we'll explore **Azure Data Lake and Storage Solutions**, including how to handle structured and unstructured data at scale, and how to build lake-centric architectures using Azure-native tools.

# Chapter 3: Exploring Azure Data Lake and Storage Solutions

## Azure Data Lake Gen2: Architecture and Features

Azure Data Lake Storage Gen2 (ADLS Gen2) is Microsoft's premier cloud storage solution built specifically for big data analytics. It combines the scalability and cost-effectiveness of Azure Blob Storage with hierarchical namespace capabilities, fine-grained security controls, and native integration with the modern Azure analytics stack. ADLS Gen2 is designed to support petabyte-scale analytics workloads efficiently and securely.

This section explores the architecture, core components, and features of ADLS Gen2. You'll learn how the system is structured, how data flows through the lake, how to manage access and governance, and how to use ADLS Gen2 in tandem with services like Azure Data Factory, Synapse Analytics, and Azure Databricks.

---

### Evolution from Gen1 to Gen2

ADLS Gen1 was Microsoft's original data lake implementation, designed for Hadoop-compatible workloads with strong security and performance. However, it was a standalone service, lacked integration with Blob Storage, and had limitations on scalability and cost-efficiency.

Gen2 was built to overcome these limitations:

- Natively built on top of **Blob Storage** (standard general-purpose v2 storage accounts).

- **Unified storage** for structured, semi-structured, and unstructured data.
- Support for both object and **hierarchical namespace**.
- Seamless integration with Azure big data analytics services.

---

## Core Architecture Components

### 1. Storage Account

Every Data Lake in Gen2 starts with a general-purpose v2 storage account. This acts as the foundation and supports both Blob and Data Lake capabilities.

You must enable **Hierarchical Namespace** when creating the storage account for Data Lake functionality.

```
az storage account create \

—name mydatalakestorage \

—resource-group datalake-rg \

—location eastus \

—sku Standard_LRS \

—kind StorageV2 \

—hierarchical-namespace true
```

**2. Containers and Directories**

- **Container**: Logical group similar to a root folder.
- **Directories**: True hierarchical structure, unlike flat Blob storage.

ADLS Gen2 supports directory-level operations (move, rename, access control), which are critical for large-scale analytics and lifecycle management.

**3. Files**

Individual data assets (e.g., CSV, Parquet, JSON, Avro). Optimized for sequential reads and writes.

## Hierarchical Namespace

One of the most important innovations in Gen2 is support for a **hierarchical namespace**. This means directories and files behave similarly to a file system:

- Native support for file-level and directory-level **ACLs**.
- More efficient **file and directory operations** (rename, delete, move).
- Enables compatibility with **Hadoop Distributed File System (HDFS)** semantics.

Comparison:

| Feature | Blob Storage (Flat) | ADLS Gen2 (Hierarchical) |
|---|---|---|
| Rename file/folder | Copy + Delete | Native rename |
| File-level ACLs | No | Yes |
| Directory navigation | Simulated | Real structure |
| Hadoop compatibility | No | Yes |

## Data Ingestion and Access

ADLS Gen2 supports multiple ingestion and access mechanisms, ensuring flexibility across different data sources and consumer tools.

**Ingestion Paths:**

- **Azure Data Factory**: Batch and streaming ETL pipelines.
- **Azure Synapse Pipelines**: Managed workflows for data movement.
- **Azure Databricks**: Streaming and batch ingestion via Spark APIs.
- **Custom Applications**: REST APIs, SDKs, or AzCopy tool.
- **Event Grid and Logic Apps**: Event-driven ingestion and transformation.

**Access Interfaces:**

- REST APIs (Blob and DFS endpoints)
- Azure Storage SDKs (.NET, Python, Java)
- Hadoop APIs via WebHDFS
- Azure Portal and Storage Explorer UI
- PowerShell, Azure CLI, and AzCopy

---

## Scalability and Performance

ADLS Gen2 is optimized for petabyte-scale workloads with billions of files. It supports high-throughput parallel processing and can elastically scale with demand.

**Performance Features:**

- Optimized for **sequential and random access.**
- Supports large file sizes (up to 5 TB).
- **Parallel writes and reads** using Spark, Hive, or MapReduce.
- Integrates with **Azure CDN** and **ExpressRoute** for faster access.

**Best Practices:**

- Use **Parquet** or **Avro** for efficient querying.

- Partition data by **date** or **category** for faster scans.
- Enable **soft delete** for recovery and data protection.

---

## Security and Access Control

Security in ADLS Gen2 is built on Azure's multi-layered protection model:

**1. Authentication**

- **Azure Active Directory (AAD)**: Identity-based access to resources.
- **Shared Access Signatures (SAS)**: Token-based delegated access.
- **Account Keys**: Legacy mechanism; not recommended for fine-grained control.

**2. Authorization**

- **Role-Based Access Control (RBAC)**: Manages access at storage account level.
- **Access Control Lists (ACLs)**: Fine-grained file and folder permissions.

Example: Set ACL using CLI

```
az storage fs access set \

—path raw/sales \
```

—acl "user::rwx,group::r—,other::—-" \

—file-system my-container \

—account-name mydatalakestorage

**3. Encryption**

- Data encrypted **at rest** using Microsoft-managed or customer-managed keys.
- Data encrypted **in transit** via HTTPS and TLS 1.2.

---

## Integration with the Azure Ecosystem

ADLS Gen2 acts as the central repository in a **Modern Data Platform** and integrates with key Azure services:

**1. Azure Synapse Analytics**

- Direct querying with **serverless SQL pools.**
- In-place querying of files (CSV, Parquet).
- Build data warehouses using Synapse Pipelines and Spark pools.

**2. Azure Data Factory**

- Ingest from over 100 sources.
- Mapping Data Flows to transform and move into curated zones.

**3. Azure Databricks**

- Supports Spark natively via dbfs:/mnt/ or abfss:// URI syntax.
- Suitable for machine learning and real-time analytics.

```
df = spark.read.parquet("abfss://raw@mydatalakestorage.dfs.core.windows.net/sales/2024/")

df.createOrReplaceTempView("sales")

spark.sql("SELECT region, SUM(amount) FROM sales GROUP BY region").show()
```

**4. Power BI**

- Connect directly or via Synapse workspaces for reporting.
- Enables real-time dashboards on top of lake data.

---

## Storage Tiers and Cost Optimization

Azure offers tiered pricing for cost-effective data management:

| Tier | Use Case | Availability | Cost |
|---|---|---|---|
| Hot | Frequently accessed data | High | Higher cost |
| Cool | Infrequently accessed data | Medium | Lower cost |
| Archive | Rarely accessed, long-term data | Low | Lowest cost |

Use **lifecycle management policies** to automate data movement:

```
{
```

```
"rules": [
{
"name": "move-old-files",
"enabled": true,
"type": "Lifecycle",
"definition": {
"filters": {
"blobTypes": ["blockBlob"],
"prefixMatch": ["raw/"]
},
"actions": {
"baseBlob": {
"tierToCool": {
"daysAfterModificationGreaterThan": 30
},
"tierToArchive": {
"daysAfterModificationGreaterThan": 180
}
}
}
```

```
}
}
]
}
```

---

## Naming and Zoning Convention

To enable effective data governance and optimize performance, data lakes typically use a **multi-zone** structure:

**1. Raw Zone**

- Ingested data in original format.
- Minimal transformation.
- Used for compliance and reproducibility.

**2. Clean/Curated Zone**

- Data cleaned, normalized, and standardized.
- Schema enforced.

**3. Enriched Zone**

- Data aggregated or joined with other sources.
- Ready for analysis and consumption.

**4. Presentation Zone**

- Optimized for BI tools.
- May include snapshots or data marts.

---

## Governance and Data Lineage

Integrate ADLS Gen2 with **Azure Purview** for governance:

- Automatically scan storage accounts.
- Apply classifications and sensitivity labels.
- Track data lineage from ingestion to reporting.

Use **tags and naming conventions** to enforce structure and ownership.

Example:

abfss://raw@datalakeeast.dfs.core.windows.net/2024/sales/uk/

abfss://clean@datalakeeast.dfs.core.windows.net/2024/sales_standardized/

---

## Summary

Azure Data Lake Storage Gen2 is a cornerstone of modern data platforms, offering a powerful combination of scalability, performance, flexibility, and integration. Its hierarchical namespace, tight security controls, and first-class compatibility with analytics engines make it ideal for enterprises looking to centralize and democratize data access across teams and departments.

Whether you're building a real-time analytics platform, training machine learning models, or implementing a global data warehouse, ADLS Gen2 provides the architecture and capabilities to meet your needs—today and into the future.

In the next section, we'll explore how to handle structured and unstructured data within ADLS Gen2, and how to design schemas and storage strategies for optimal performance and cost efficiency.

## Storing Structured and Unstructured Data

Azure Data Lake Storage Gen2 (ADLS Gen2) offers a flexible and powerful platform for storing and managing both structured and unstructured data at scale. In today's data-driven environments, organizations collect a wide variety of data types—from transactional records and telemetry logs to multimedia files and real-time streams. Storing this data efficiently and in a format conducive to processing and analysis is critical to the success of any modern data architecture.

This section explores the strategies, formats, and tools for ingesting, storing, and organizing both structured and unstructured data within ADLS Gen2. We will cover data types, common storage formats, partitioning strategies, naming conventions, compression techniques, and performance optimization for different data scenarios.

## Understanding Structured vs. Unstructured Data

### Structured Data

Structured data is organized in predefined schemas, usually in rows and columns. It is highly searchable and can be stored in formats like CSV, Parquet, Avro, or relational databases.

**Examples:**

- Financial transactions
- Inventory records
- Sensor readings
- Customer profiles

### Unstructured Data

Unstructured data does not follow a specific data model and is typically stored in its raw form. It may contain text, multimedia, or semi-structured data formats.

**Examples:**

- Video and audio files
- PDFs and Word documents
- Emails
- JSON logs

**Semi-Structured Data**

Data that does not reside in a relational table but still contains some organizational properties.

**Examples:**

- XML
- JSON
- YAML
- NoSQL document formats

---

## File Formats for Data Storage

ADLS Gen2 supports a wide range of formats. Choosing the right format affects performance, cost, and downstream compatibility.

**Structured Formats**

| Format | Description | Use Case |
|---|---|---|
| CSV | Simple, readable text format; no schema | Lightweight exports, compatibility |
| Parquet | Columnar, compressed, efficient for read-heavy workloads | Analytics, batch processing |
| Avro | Row-based, compact, schema evolution support | Streaming, write-heavy workloads |
| ORC | Columnar format optimized for Hive | Large-scale analytics |

**Example: Storing Parquet Files**

```
df.write.parquet("abfss://curated@datalakestorage.dfs.core.windows.net/
sales/2024/")
```

Parquet provides significant performance benefits when reading specific columns or working with tools like Synapse and Spark.

**Unstructured Formats**

| Format | Description | Use Case |
|---|---|---|
| .txt/.log | Free-form logs and text | Application logs |
| .jpg/.png | Image files | Document scanning |
| .mp4/.mp3 | Multimedia | Surveillance, audio |
| .pdf/.docx | Office documents | Contracts, reports |

Stored as binary files within ADLS, unstructured data is often tagged and cataloged for discoverability.

## Best Practices for Structured Data Storage

### 1. Use Optimized File Formats

Prefer **Parquet** or **Avro** for storing structured data due to:

- Built-in compression
- Schema support
- High-speed querying via columnar access

### 2. Apply Partitioning

Partitioning divides data into logical units (e.g., by date, region) to improve read performance.

**Example Partition Path:**

abfss://curated@datalakestorage.dfs.core.windows.net/sales/year=2024/month=04/region=uk/

Partition pruning by query engines reduces scan size and speeds up analytics.

**3. Avoid Small Files (File Fragmentation)**

Spark and Synapse perform poorly on millions of tiny files. Aim for file sizes between **256 MB – 1 GB**.

**Solutions:**

- Merge small files periodically using batch jobs.
- Use **Auto Loader** in Databricks for streaming ingestion with auto-batching.

---

## Best Practices for Unstructured Data Storage

**1. Organize with Metadata Directories**

Unstructured files should be stored in directory structures that reflect metadata dimensions such as source, date, or document type.

**Example:**

abfss://raw@datalakestorage.dfs.core.windows.net/documents/legal/contracts/2025/

### 2. Use Tags or External Metadata Catalogs

Since binary files lack native schemas, use Azure Purview or a custom metadata repository to catalog:

- File type
- Owner
- Classification
- Sensitivity level
- Retention policy

### 3. Enable Soft Delete and Versioning

Protect data integrity and support recovery.

az storage blob service-properties delete-policy update \

—account-name datalakeaccount \

—enable true \

—days-retained 30

---

## Compression and Encoding

Compression reduces storage costs and I/O but must be chosen based on use case compatibility.

| Format | Compression | Best For |
|---|---|---|
| Parquet | Snappy | Analytics workloads |
| Avro | Deflate | Event logs |
| CSV | Gzip | Archives |

### File Encoding

Always use **UTF-8** for text-based files. Consistent encoding avoids downstream processing errors in Spark or SQL-based tools.

## Ingesting Structured and Unstructured Data

### Using Azure Data Factory

**Structured Ingestion Example:**

- Source: SQL Server on-prem
- Sink: Parquet files in ADLS Gen2

Steps:

1. Define Linked Services for source and sink.
2. Use Mapping Data Flows to transform.
3. Set partitioning rules on sink.

**Unstructured Ingestion Example:**

- Source: SFTP server with documents
- Sink: Raw zone in ADLS Gen2

ADF provides built-in connectors and binary copy functionality to handle these files efficiently.

**Using AzCopy for Bulk Upload**

```
azcopy copy "./localfolder/*" "https://datalakestorage.dfs.core.windows.net/raw/documents/"—recursive
```

## Integration with Processing Tools

ADLS Gen2 is tightly integrated with Azure's analytics services to handle diverse workloads.

**Azure Synapse Analytics**

- Read/write from files using **serverless SQL**:

```
SELECT *

FROM OPENROWSET(

BULK 'https://datalakestorage.dfs.core.windows.net/curated/sales/2024/*.parquet',

FORMAT='PARQUET'

) AS sales
```

- Supports pushdown predicates and column pruning.

**Azure Databricks**

- Spark-native reading of semi-structured JSON or Parquet:

```
df = spark.read.option("multiline", "true").json("abfss://raw@datalakestorage.dfs.core.windows.net/iot/2024/")

df.printSchema()
```

- Process and store output in curated zones.

---

## Data Lifecycle and Archival Strategy

To maintain cost efficiency and compliance, define policies that manage how long data is stored, where it moves, and when it is deleted.

**Example Lifecycle:**

- **Raw Zone**: 90 days retention
- **Curated Zone**: 1 year
- **Archive Zone**: 7 years (regulatory)

Use automated lifecycle policies to enforce:

```
{
"rules": [
{
"name": "archive-old-logs",
"enabled": true,
"type": "Lifecycle",
```

```
"definition": {
"filters": {
"blobTypes": ["blockBlob"],
"prefixMatch": ["raw/logs/"]
},
"actions": {
"baseBlob": {
"tierToCool": {
"daysAfterModificationGreaterThan": 30
},
"tierToArchive": {
"daysAfterModificationGreaterThan": 180
}
}
}
}
}
]
}
```

## Organizing Your Data Lake

Adopt a consistent and scalable folder structure. Example:

/<zone>/<data-domain>/<data-product>/<yyyy>/<MM>/<dd>/

**Example:**

/curated/retail/transactions/2025/04/25/

This structure supports efficient scanning, discoverability, and governance.

---

## Summary

Storing structured and unstructured data in Azure Data Lake Storage Gen2 requires thoughtful planning and adherence to best practices. From choosing optimal file formats and compression methods to partitioning and organizing data using metadata, every decision impacts performance, cost, and scalability.

ADLS Gen2's support for hierarchical namespaces, scalable architecture, and deep integration with Azure analytics tools makes it the perfect foundation for enterprise data lakes. Whether you're dealing with time-series IoT data or large-scale document archives, the platform provides the capabilities needed to ingest, store, query, and manage data at cloud scale.

The next section will explore how to integrate ADLS Gen2 with Azure Data Factory and Synapse to build automated, scalable, and secure data pipelines.

# Integration with Data Factory and Synapse

Integrating Azure Data Lake Storage Gen2 (ADLS Gen2) with Azure Data Factory (ADF) and Azure Synapse Analytics forms the backbone of modern, scalable, and fully automated data pipelines in the cloud. This integration enables end-to-end workflows that ingest, transform, store, analyze, and visualize data using a unified set of Azure-native tools.

This section delves into how ADLS Gen2 is integrated with ADF for data movement and transformation, and with Synapse for analytics and reporting. It covers use cases, architecture patterns, implementation steps, and best practices for real-world data pipeline scenarios, including both batch and near real-time data processing.

## Benefits of Integration

The integration between ADLS Gen2, ADF, and Synapse provides the following key benefits:

- **Unified data platform**: Seamless orchestration, storage, and analytics within a single ecosystem.
- **Scalability**: Automatically scale data processing with parallelism and elastic compute.
- **Security**: Integrated access control using Azure Active Directory and managed identities.
- **Efficiency**: Optimize cost and performance using tiered storage, partitioned data, and serverless querying.

## Core Integration Architecture

### Typical Data Flow:

1. **Ingest**: Data Factory ingests raw data from diverse sources

(databases, APIs, files, IoT).

2. **Store**: Raw data is stored in the raw zone of ADLS Gen2.
3. **Transform**: Mapping Data Flows or Synapse pipelines perform transformations.
4. **Curate**: Cleaned data is stored in curated/enriched zones.
5. **Analyze**: Synapse SQL or Spark pools query the curated data.
6. **Visualize**: Power BI reads results via Synapse or directly from the lake.

---

## Ingesting Data with Azure Data Factory

Azure Data Factory is a fully managed ETL/ELT service. It supports 100+ connectors and can copy, transform, and orchestrate data pipelines.

### Creating a Linked Service to ADLS Gen2

```
{

"name": "AzureDataLakeStorage1",

"type": "LinkedService",

"typeProperties": {

"url": "https://<your-storage-account>.dfs.core.windows.net",

"servicePrincipalId": "<client-id>",

"servicePrincipalKey": "<client-secret>",

"tenant": "<tenant-id>"

}
```

```
}
```

Alternatively, use **Managed Identity** for a more secure approach:

- Assign Storage Blob Data Contributor role to the ADF managed identity.
- No secrets required in code.

**Copying Data to ADLS Gen2**

ADF Copy Activities can ingest data from sources like:

- SQL Server
- Blob Storage
- SFTP
- REST APIs

**Example pipeline**:

1. Source: On-prem SQL database (via Self-hosted IR).
2. Sink: Parquet files in ADLS Gen2.

```
{
"type": "Copy",
"inputs": [{"name": "SqlTableDataset"}],
"outputs": [{"name": "AdlsParquetDataset"}],
"typeProperties": {
```

```
"source": {
"type": "SqlSource"
},
"sink": {
"type": "ParquetSink"
}
}
}
```

**Using Mapping Data Flows**

For data transformation:

- Visual UI for cleaning, pivoting, joining, aggregating.
- Outputs to ADLS in multiple formats (Parquet, CSV, JSON).

**Common transformations**:

- Remove duplicates.
- Standardize date formats.
- Join customer and order tables.

## Integrating with Azure Synapse Analytics

Azure Synapse Analytics is a cloud-native analytics platform that allows both big data and data warehousing capabilities.

### 1. Reading Files from ADLS Gen2

Use **serverless SQL pools** for on-demand querying:

```
SELECT *
FROM OPENROWSET(
BULK 'https://<storage-account>.dfs.core.windows.net/curated/sales/2025/',
FORMAT='PARQUET'
) AS sales_data;
```

### 2. Dedicated SQL Pools

- Ideal for structured datasets that require fast, interactive queries.
- Use **PolyBase** to load data from ADLS into relational tables.

```
CREATE EXTERNAL DATA SOURCE SalesData
WITH (
TYPE = HADOOP,
LOCATION = 'abfss://curated@<account>.dfs.core.windows.net/'
```

```
);
CREATE EXTERNAL FILE FORMAT ParquetFormat
WITH (
FORMAT_TYPE = PARQUET
);
CREATE EXTERNAL TABLE Sales
(
OrderID INT,
CustomerID INT,
Amount FLOAT,
OrderDate DATE
)
WITH (
LOCATION='/sales/2025/',
DATA_SOURCE = SalesData,
FILE_FORMAT = ParquetFormat
);
```

**3. Apache Spark Pools**

- Use Spark notebooks to read/write data to ADLS.

- Suitable for machine learning, complex transformations.

```
df =
spark.read.parquet("abfss://curated@<account>.dfs.core.windows.net/
sales/2025/")

df.filter(df["Amount"] >
100).write.mode("overwrite").parquet("abfss://enriched@<account>.df
highvalue/")
```

---

## Real-Time and Near Real-Time Integration

For time-sensitive workloads, integration can be extended to include:

- **Event Hubs or IoT Hub** as ingestion sources.
- **Stream Analytics** or **Databricks Structured Streaming** for real-time processing.
- Writing output to ADLS Gen2 for further downstream analytics in Synapse.

---

## Orchestration Patterns

ADF and Synapse pipelines support sophisticated orchestration capabilities:

- **Triggers**: Schedule-based, tumbling window, event-based.
- **Control flow**: If conditions, loops, dependencies.

- **Monitoring**: Visual pipeline run history, alerts, logging.

**Example pattern**:

1. Trigger every hour.
2. Run Copy Activity to ingest new data.
3. Run Mapping Data Flow to clean.
4. Run Stored Procedure in Synapse to update summary table.

---

## Security and Access Control

Ensure secure integration:

- Use **Managed Identity** for ADF and Synapse access to ADLS.

- Set **RBAC** at the storage account level.

- Use **Access Control Lists (ACLs)** for granular access to folders/files.

- Enable **firewall** and **Private Endpoints** for networking security.

```
az storage fs access set \

—path curated/sales \

—acl "user::<object-id>:rwx,group::r—,other::—-" \

—file-system curated \

—account-name mydatalake
```

## Monitoring and Cost Management

### Data Factory Monitoring

- View pipeline runs and activity duration.
- Export logs to Log Analytics for audit trails.

### Synapse Monitoring

- Use **Monitor Hub** for job history, query plans.
- Enable **SQL Analytics** in Azure Monitor.

### Cost Tips

- Use **Parquet** format to minimize query scan size.
- Use **serverless pools** for ad-hoc querying.
- Compress files during ingestion.
- Archive old data using tiered storage policies.

---

## Example End-to-End Use Case

### Retail Sales Reporting Platform

1. **Ingest**: Data Factory pulls hourly sales data from on-prem SQL to ADLS Gen2 (raw zone).
2. **Transform**: Mapping Data Flows clean and standardize into curated zone.
3. **Enrich**: Join sales with customer data using Synapse Spark

pool.

4. **Analyze**: Serverless SQL pool queries generate KPIs.
5. **Visualize**: Power BI dashboards refresh using Synapse datasets.
6. **Govern**: Azure Purview catalogs datasets and enforces classification.

---

## Summary

The integration of Azure Data Lake Storage Gen2 with Azure Data Factory and Synapse Analytics creates a cohesive and powerful data ecosystem capable of handling everything from real-time ingestion to enterprise-scale analytics. By adopting best practices in design, orchestration, security, and monitoring, organizations can build resilient data pipelines that meet both current and future needs.

This integration enables a true data lakehouse architecture, where structured and unstructured data can coexist, be governed, and analyzed with ease. In the next section, we'll dive deeper into data governance strategies, access control configurations, and best practices for managing data quality and compliance within ADLS Gen2.

# Access Control and Data Governance

As organizations increasingly rely on data lakes for enterprise-wide data storage and analytics, implementing robust access control and data governance becomes essential. Azure Data Lake Storage Gen2 (ADLS Gen2) provides comprehensive features for managing data access, enforcing security policies, auditing activity, and ensuring compliance with regulatory and corporate standards.

This section explores the various mechanisms available in ADLS Gen2 for enforcing access control, managing data governance, securing sensitive data, and aligning with best practices for data quality, privacy, and lifecycle management. By understanding and applying these practices, organizations can maintain the integrity and accountability of their data platform at scale.

## Access Control in ADLS Gen2

ADLS Gen2 provides two main access control models:

1. **Role-Based Access Control (RBAC)**
2. **Access Control Lists (ACLs)**

These models can be used individually or together to enforce layered, fine-grained permissions.

## Role-Based Access Control (RBAC)

RBAC is enforced at the **Azure Resource Manager (ARM)** level. It controls access to the storage account and containers.

**Common Roles:**

| Role Name | Permissions |
|---|---|
| Storage Account Contributor | Full control over the storage account |
| Storage Blob Data Contributor | Read/write/delete data in containers |
| Storage Blob Data Reader | Read-only access to blob data |
| Storage Blob Data Owner | Full data-level permissions including ACLs and metadata |
| Storage Blob Delegator | Required for AAD-based access via OAuth |

**Assigning a Role with Azure CLI:**

```
az role assignment create \

—assignee <user-or-group-object-id> \

—role "Storage Blob Data Contributor" \

—scope
/subscriptions/<sub-id>/resourceGroups/<rg-name>/providers/Microsoft.Storage/storageAccounts/<storage-account-name>
```

**RBAC Limitations:**

- Coarse-grained (container or account level).
- Does not apply to individual directories or files.

---

## Access Control Lists (ACLs)

ACLs are POSIX-style permissions applied directly to directories and files. They enable granular access control within the hierarchical namespace of ADLS Gen2.

**ACL Components:**

- user:: – Permissions for the owner of the object.
- group:: – Permissions for users in the object's group.
- other:: – Permissions for everyone else.
- default: – Applied to new child objects within a directory.

**Example ACL Entry:**

```
user::rwx,group::r—,other::—-

default:user::rwx,default:group::r—,default:other::—-
```

**Setting ACLs with CLI:**

```
az storage fs access set \

—acl "user::rwx,group::r—,other::—-" \

—path "curated/sales" \

—file-system curated \

—account-name mydatalake
```

**Best Practice:** Use **default ACLs** on directories to automatically assign access permissions to newly created files and subdirectories.

---

## Combining RBAC and ACLs

RBAC controls **who** can access the storage account; ACLs control **what** they can do inside the filesystem.

| Scope | Control Type | Tool |
|---|---|---|
| Storage Account | RBAC | Azure Portal, CLI |
| Filesystem Level | ACL | CLI, REST, SDK |

**Example Use Case:**

- Grant read-only RBAC at storage account.
- Use ACLs to allow specific directories to be writable for specific teams.

---

## Data Classification and Sensitivity Labels

Understanding the nature of your data is critical for compliance and risk management. Azure provides tools to automatically scan, classify, and label data.

### Azure Purview Integration

Azure Purview (Microsoft Purview) provides unified data governance and allows:

- Scanning ADLS Gen2 for sensitive data (e.g., PII, PHI).
- Applying labels and classifications.

- Tracking data lineage and impact analysis.
- Delegating stewardship responsibilities.

**Examples of Classification Types:**

| Classification | Description |
|---|---|
| Personally Identifiable Information (PII) | Names, emails, SSNs |
| Financial Data | Credit card numbers, account info |
| Health Information | Diagnoses, prescriptions |

**Enabling Scan in Azure Purview:**

1. Register your ADLS Gen2 account.
2. Configure scanning rules and frequency.
3. Apply policies or alerts for labeled datasets.

---

## Auditing and Logging

Tracking access and changes to data is essential for operational security and compliance.

**Options for Auditing:**

1. **Storage Analytics Logs**
2. **Azure Monitor / Diagnostic Settings**
3. **Log Analytics Workspace**
4. **Microsoft Sentinel (SIEM Integration)**

**Enabling Diagnostic Logs:**

```
az monitor diagnostic-settings create \

—resource
/subscriptions/<sub-id>/resourceGroups/<rg>/providers/
Microsoft.Storage/storageAccounts/<account> \

—name "audit-logs" \

—workspace <log-analytics-workspace-id> \

—logs '[{"category": "StorageRead", "enabled": true}, {"category":
"StorageWrite", "enabled": true}]'
```

**Sample KQL Query:**

```
StorageBlobLogs

| where OperationName == "GetBlob"

| summarize Count = count() by CallerIpAddress, Identity,
TimeGenerated
```

Use alerts to trigger actions or notify teams when sensitive data is accessed or modified.

---

## Data Retention and Lifecycle Policies

Managing the lifecycle of data is a key part of governance. ADLS Gen2 supports automated rules to transition or delete files based on age, access, or tags.

**Example Use Cases:**

- Move unused data from Hot to Cool/Archive.
- Delete logs after 90 days to save costs.
- Retain regulatory datasets for 7 years.

**Enabling a Lifecycle Management Policy:**

```
{
"rules": [
{
"name": "delete-raw-data",
"enabled": true,
"type": "Lifecycle",
"definition": {
"filters": {
"blobTypes": ["blockBlob"],
"prefixMatch": ["raw/"]
},
"actions": {
"baseBlob": {
"delete": {
```

```
"daysAfterModificationGreaterThan": 90
}
}
}
}
}
]
}
```

## Data Quality and Lineage

Governance also means tracking the **origin**, **transformations**, and **quality** of your data.

**Strategies for Quality:**

- Apply validation logic in Data Factory or Synapse pipelines.
- Tag records with error statuses or quality scores.
- Build retry pipelines for corrupt files.

**Tools for Lineage:**

- **Azure Purview**: Shows data origin, transformation flow.

- **Synapse Pipelines**: Track activities and datasets through lineage views.

**Example Flow:**

1. Ingest raw sales files.
2. Standardize fields and remove duplicates.
3. Join with reference data.
4. Produce a final curated dataset.

Each step is logged and available for traceability.

## Data Stewardship and Governance Roles

Effective data governance depends not only on tools but also on people.

**Key Roles:**

| Role | Responsibilities |
|---|---|
| Data Owner | Defines access policies, ensures data quality |
| Data Steward | Maintains metadata, classification, lineage |
| Security Admin | Configures access controls and audits |
| Data Engineer | Implements ETL and data flow logic |
| Compliance Officer | Ensures alignment with regulatory frameworks |

Define responsibilities clearly and align them with Azure role assignments.

## Regulatory Compliance Alignment

ADLS Gen2 can help satisfy compliance requirements for:

- **GDPR**: Right to erasure, consent tracking, encryption at rest.
- **HIPAA**: Audit trails, data access monitoring, secure sharing.
- **CCPA**: Consumer data access, labeling, deletion automation.
- **ISO 27001, SOC 2**: Infrastructure compliance, access control.

Use **Microsoft Compliance Manager** to map technical configurations to compliance controls.

---

## Summary

Access control and governance are foundational pillars of any secure and trustworthy data platform. With Azure Data Lake Storage Gen2, organizations are equipped with powerful, flexible tools to enforce precise access policies, classify and track sensitive data, and automate data lifecycle operations.

Combining Role-Based Access Control (RBAC), Access Control Lists (ACLs), metadata classification, and monitoring tools like Azure Monitor and Purview, organizations can build a governance framework that not only protects their data but also makes it more discoverable, auditable, and valuable.

In the next chapter, we'll explore Azure Synapse Analytics in depth—covering architecture, core components, and how it integrates seamlessly with ADLS Gen2 to power scalable, unified analytics at cloud speed.

# Chapter 4: Introduction to Azure Synapse Analytics

## What is Synapse Analytics?

Azure Synapse Analytics is an integrated analytics platform that enables organizations to ingest, prepare, manage, and serve data for immediate business intelligence and machine learning needs. It brings together big data and data warehousing into a unified experience, eliminating the traditional silos between operational data stores and analytical platforms.

Synapse empowers data professionals—including data engineers, data analysts, and data scientists—to collaborate in a single workspace with unified security, scalable compute, and seamless connectivity to various data sources, especially Azure Data Lake Storage Gen2. This section offers an in-depth overview of what Synapse is, what problems it solves, and how it fits into the broader Azure data ecosystem.

---

### Key Capabilities of Azure Synapse Analytics

Synapse is not just a data warehouse. It is an end-to-end analytics service that includes:

1. **Synapse SQL**: Offers both on-demand (serverless) and provisioned (dedicated) query processing engines for SQL-based analytics.
2. **Apache Spark Integration**: Built-in Spark pools for large-scale distributed data processing.
3. **Pipelines**: Data orchestration and integration using a visual interface similar to Azure Data Factory.

4. **Data Explorer**: Kusto-like query experience for log and telemetry analytics.
5. **Studio Experience**: Web-based development environment for SQL, Spark, and orchestration.
6. **Security and Monitoring**: Integrated access control, auditing, and monitoring through Azure Monitor.

---

## Challenges Synapse Addresses

Before Synapse, organizations often had to use multiple tools for:

- Ingesting data from operational stores
- Storing raw and curated data
- Performing big data processing and transformation
- Querying structured data warehouses
- Visualizing data in BI tools

This disjointed architecture resulted in:

- Data silos
- High operational overhead
- Slow time-to-insight
- Security inconsistencies

Synapse unifies these components into a single, secure, and scalable platform.

---

## The Synapse Workspace

A Synapse workspace is the control plane where all components are managed.

**Core elements within a Synapse workspace:**

- **Linked Services**: Connections to external data sources like ADLS, SQL Server, Cosmos DB.
- **Datasets**: Metadata representations of data sources.
- **Pipelines**: ETL and orchestration workflows.
- **Notebooks**: Spark-based interactive code environments.
- **SQL Scripts**: T-SQL based queries using either serverless or dedicated pools.
- **Integration Runtime (IR)**: Compute infrastructure for running data movement and transformation.

---

## Serverless vs. Dedicated SQL Pools

### Serverless SQL Pools

- **No infrastructure setup required**
- Ideal for ad-hoc exploration
- Cost based on data scanned (pay-per-query)

**Example Query:**

```
SELECT *
FROM OPENROWSET(
BULK 'https://datalake.dfs.core.windows.net/curated/sales/2025/*.parquet',
FORMAT = 'PARQUET'
) AS sales
WHERE sales.Region = 'Europe';
```

**Dedicated SQL Pools**

- **Pre-allocated, provisioned resources**
- Best for predictable, high-volume workloads
- Supports indexing, materialized views, and performance tuning

**Provisioning via CLI:**

```
az synapse sql pool create \
—name salesdw \
—workspace-name synapseworkspace \
—resource-group analytics-rg \
—performance-level DW100c
```

## Apache Spark Integration

Synapse provides built-in Spark pools for big data workloads, making it suitable for:

- ETL transformations
- Real-time analytics
- Machine learning pipelines

**Key Features:**

- Notebooks in PySpark, Scala, SparkSQL, and .NET for Spark
- Shared metadata via workspace databases
- Integration with ML libraries and external packages

**Example: Reading from ADLS Gen2**

```
df = spark.read.parquet("abfss://curated@datalake.dfs.core.windows.net/sales/2025/")

df.createOrReplaceTempView("sales")

spark.sql("SELECT region, SUM(amount) FROM sales GROUP BY region").show()
```

---

## Synapse Pipelines

Pipelines in Synapse mirror Azure Data Factory capabilities with visual ETL authoring. Use them to orchestrate:

- Data ingestion from APIs, databases, files
- Transformation using Mapping Data Flows or Spark jobs
- Data loading into dedicated SQL or downstream systems

**Example Activities:**

- Copy Activity: Move data from SQL to Parquet in ADLS
- Data Flow Activity: Standardize date formats and correct nulls
- Notebook Activity: Run a Spark job for advanced processing

---

## Unified Security Model

Synapse offers integrated security across all components:

- **Azure Active Directory (AAD)** authentication
- **Managed Private Endpoints** to access secure data stores
- **Column-level and row-level security** in dedicated SQL pools
- **Dynamic data masking** to protect sensitive columns

- **Auditing and threat detection** via Microsoft Defender for Cloud

**Granting Access via AAD:**

```
az synapse role assignment create \
—workspace-name synapseworkspace \
—role "Synapse Contributor" \
—assignee <user-object-id>
```

## Monitoring and Diagnostics

Synapse includes built-in monitoring tools and integrates with Azure Monitor for broader observability.

**Metrics Tracked:**

- Query execution time
- Data movement duration
- Pipeline success/failure
- Resource utilization

**Diagnostic Logs Can Be Sent To:**

- Log Analytics
- Event Hub
- Azure Storage

**Sample KQL Query (in Log Analytics):**

```
SynapsePipelineRuns
| where Status == "Failed"
| summarize count() by PipelineName, bin(TimeGenerated, 1h)
```

## Integration with External Services

Azure Synapse connects with a wide variety of services:

- **Power BI**: Direct connection to Synapse SQL pools
- **Azure Data Lake Storage**: Native read/write support
- **Azure Machine Learning**: Model scoring and training
- **Azure Purview**: Data cataloging and lineage tracking
- **GitHub/Azure DevOps**: CI/CD integration for versioning pipelines and scripts

---

## Key Use Cases

### 1. Enterprise Data Warehousing

- Consolidate data from various sources
- Optimize queries using partitioning and materialized views
- Govern data with RBAC and Purview

**2. Big Data Transformation**

- Use Spark pools to process billions of records
- Perform join/merge/filter operations at scale
- Write curated outputs back to ADLS Gen2

**3. Real-Time Analytics**

- Ingest data with Synapse Pipelines or Event Hubs
- Use Spark Streaming or serverless SQL for immediate insights
- Build dashboards with Power BI

**4. Machine Learning Integration**

- Prepare features with Spark
- Train models using SynapseML or Azure ML
- Score results and store predictions in Synapse tables

---

## Advantages of Using Synapse

| Feature | Benefit |
|---|---|
| Unified platform | No need for separate tools for ETL, querying, and storage |
| Scalability | Handles petabyte-scale data workloads |
| Flexible compute options | Choose between on-demand and provisioned models |
| Built-in security and governance | Integrated with AAD, Purview, and Defender |
| Cost efficiency | Pay-as-you-go for serverless or fixed cost for dedicated |

## Summary

Azure Synapse Analytics represents a transformational shift in how organizations approach data analytics. By unifying SQL, Spark, data integration, and governance into a single, powerful platform, Synapse eliminates complexity and accelerates time-to-insight.

Whether your goal is to modernize an existing data warehouse, unlock the value of unstructured data, or operationalize machine learning at scale, Synapse provides the tools, scalability, and flexibility to get there efficiently and securely.

In the next section, we will explore the **architecture and core components** of Synapse Analytics, including how data flows through the system and how compute, storage, and orchestration components interact.

# Architecture and Core Components

Azure Synapse Analytics is architected as a unified platform that brings together data ingestion, storage, processing, integration, and visualization into a single workspace. Understanding the architecture and core components of Synapse Analytics is key to designing scalable, secure, and efficient solutions for diverse analytics workloads.

This section provides a detailed breakdown of Synapse's modular architecture, including its compute and storage models, data integration engine, workspace components, security layers, and how they interact to support batch and real-time data processing.

## High-Level Architecture Overview

At a high level, Azure Synapse Analytics integrates five core architectural layers:

1. **Data Storage Layer** – Persistent storage using Azure Data Lake Storage Gen2.
2. **Compute Layer** – Dedicated SQL, Serverless SQL, and Apache Spark pools.
3. **Orchestration Layer** – Synapse Pipelines for data movement and scheduling.
4. **Development Environment** – Synapse Studio for unified analytics authoring.
5. **Security & Governance** – Role-based access control, auditing, encryption, and data classification.

Together, these layers form a cohesive analytics environment that can serve structured and unstructured data processing needs across data engineering, analytics, and machine learning domains.

## 1. Storage Layer: Azure Data Lake Integration

Synapse Analytics is tightly coupled with **Azure Data Lake Storage Gen2** (ADLS Gen2), which serves as the default storage layer for all assets.

**Features:**

- Store raw, curated, and modeled data in a hierarchical namespace.
- Store datasets in formats like Parquet, CSV, Avro, JSON.
- Native access through both Spark and SQL engines.

**Storage Account Setup Example:**

```
az storage account create \
—name synapsestorage \
—resource-group analytics-rg \
—location eastus \
—sku Standard_LRS \
—kind StorageV2 \
—hierarchical-namespace true
```

Synapse uses a **primary storage account** when the workspace is created. Additional linked storage accounts can also be added.

## 2. Compute Layer

Synapse provides multiple compute engines tailored for different workloads:

### a. Dedicated SQL Pools

- Formerly known as SQL Data Warehouse.
- Pre-provisioned compute (DWUs or cDWU).
- Used for structured data and dimensional modeling.
- Optimized for high-performance batch queries.

**Key Features:**

- Partitioning, distribution strategies
- Materialized views
- Indexes and statistics
- PolyBase for data ingestion

### b. Serverless SQL Pools

- On-demand compute.
- No infrastructure to manage.
- Ideal for ad-hoc queries over files in ADLS.

**Example:**

SELECT TOP 100 *

```
FROM OPENROWSET(
BULK 'https://synapsestorage.dfs.core.windows.net/curated/sales/*.parquet',
FORMAT='PARQUET'
) AS rows
```

**c. Apache Spark Pools**

- Supports batch, streaming, and machine learning tasks.
- Works well with unstructured/semi-structured data (e.g., JSON, text, images).
- Fully integrated with the Synapse workspace.

**Languages Supported:**

- PySpark
- Scala
- Spark SQL
- .NET for Spark

**Cluster Configuration:** You can define executor size, node count, and autoscaling during Spark pool creation.

**d. Data Explorer Pools (Optional)**

- Optimized for log and telemetry analytics.

- Kusto Query Language (KQL) support.
- Great for time-series and operational analytics.

---

## 3. Orchestration Layer: Synapse Pipelines

The orchestration layer allows you to build data workflows using visual components or code.

**Capabilities:**

- Connect to 100+ sources via Linked Services.
- Orchestrate batch and streaming pipelines.
- Trigger execution based on time, events, or dependencies.

**Pipeline Activities:**

- Data movement: Copy Activity
- Data transformation: Data Flows, Notebooks
- Control flow: ForEach, Switch, Wait, Web

**Example: Copy from Blob to Synapse Table**

```
{
"name": "CopyToSynapse",
"type": "Copy",
"typeProperties": {
```

```
"source": {
"type": "DelimitedTextSource"
},
"sink": {
"type": "SqlSink",
"preCopyScript": "TRUNCATE TABLE [staging].[sales]"
}
}
}
```

## 4. Synapse Studio: Unified Development Interface

Synapse Studio is the browser-based IDE for authoring, managing, and monitoring all Synapse artifacts.

**Features:**

- Develop SQL scripts and Spark notebooks.
- Design data flows and pipelines visually.
- Browse data in linked storage and databases.
- Monitor execution and resource usage.
- Publish to Git integration for source control.

**Key Development Areas:**

- **Data Hub**: Explore data lakes, databases, linked services.
- **Develop Hub**: Create scripts, notebooks, pipelines.
- **Integrate Hub**: Manage pipeline orchestration.
- **Monitor Hub**: View logs, errors, and execution history.
- **Manage Hub**: Configure security, pools, and integration runtimes.

---

## 5. Security and Governance

Security is embedded into every layer of Synapse architecture.

### a. Authentication and Access Control

- Azure Active Directory-based access.
- Role-Based Access Control (RBAC) within workspace and data level.
- Managed private endpoints for VNet isolation.

### b. Data Encryption

- Encryption at rest with Microsoft-managed or customer-managed keys.
- Encryption in transit enforced via TLS 1.2.

**c. Auditing and Threat Detection**

- Integration with Azure Monitor and Microsoft Defender.
- Audit logs can be streamed to Log Analytics or Event Hub.

**Sample Role Assignment:**

```
az synapse role assignment create \
—workspace-name synapseworkspace \
—role "Synapse SQL Administrator" \
—assignee <user-object-id>
```

## Workspace Databases

Synapse supports two database types:

1. **SQL On-Demand (serverless)**: Used to define metadata over external files.
2. **Dedicated SQL**: Traditional relational databases backed by provisioned resources.

Both support T-SQL but differ in capabilities, performance, and cost model.

**Example External Table Definition:**

```
CREATE EXTERNAL TABLE Sales (
OrderID INT,
```

```
OrderDate DATE,
Amount FLOAT
)
WITH (
LOCATION = '/sales/2025/',
DATA_SOURCE = SalesLake,
FILE_FORMAT = ParquetFormat
);
```

## Integration Runtimes

Integration Runtime (IR) is the compute infrastructure for data movement and transformation.

- **AutoResolve IR**: Default IR for most operations.
- **Azure IR**: Used for cloud-based copy activities.
- **Self-Hosted IR**: Required for accessing on-prem or private networks.

You can monitor IR performance and scale as needed depending on the job's size and frequency.

## Performance Optimization Layers

Synapse supports multiple performance tuning mechanisms:

- **Partitioning**: Split data by values (e.g., date) for parallel query execution.

- **Distribution Methods**: Hash, Round-robin, Replicated.
- **Materialized Views**: Cache computed results to speed up recurring queries.
- **Resource Classes**: Prioritize workloads by allocating more/less memory.

**Optimizing Distribution Example:**

```
CREATE TABLE Sales (
OrderID INT,
CustomerID INT,
Amount FLOAT
)
WITH (
DISTRIBUTION = HASH(CustomerID),
CLUSTERED COLUMNSTORE INDEX
);
```

## Real-Time and Streaming Architecture

Synapse supports near real-time analytics using Spark Structured Streaming or ingestion pipelines from Event Hubs or IoT Hub.

**Architecture Example:**

- IoT Hub ingests device telemetry.

- Event Hub feeds streaming data to Spark.
- Transformed data is stored in ADLS and queried by serverless SQL.

---

## Architecture Summary Diagram (Descriptive)

```
+———————————————————+
| Azure Synapse Studio |
| - SQL Scripts |
| - Spark Notebooks |
| - Pipelines |
| - Monitoring |
+————————+——————————+
|
v
+————————+——————————+
| Compute Pools |
| - Dedicated SQL |
| - Serverless SQL |
| - Apache Spark |
| - Data Explorer |
+————————+——————————+
```

```
|
v
+————————+—————————+
| Storage Layer |
| - ADLS Gen2 |
| - External Linked Sources |
+————————+—————————+
|
v
+————————+—————————+
| Governance & Security |
| - RBAC & ACLs |
| - Encryption |
| - Monitoring & Logging |
+————————————————-+
```

## Summary

The architecture of Azure Synapse Analytics is designed to unify diverse analytics workloads under a single, secure, and scalable platform. By integrating a rich storage layer with flexible compute engines, visual orchestration tools, and enterprise-grade security, Synapse empowers organizations to streamline data operations and accelerate time-to-insight.

Whether your goal is to ingest streaming telemetry, transform big data in Spark, run high-performance SQL queries, or orchestrate complex data flows, Synapse provides the infrastructure and tools to support it all—from one cohesive workspace.

In the next section, we'll explore the differences between **Synapse SQL and Spark Pools**, diving deeper into when and how to use each engine effectively.

# Synapse SQL vs Spark Pools

Azure Synapse Analytics provides multiple compute engines to accommodate a variety of analytics workloads—primarily **Synapse SQL** and **Apache Spark pools**. Each engine is optimized for specific use cases, and understanding when and how to use them is essential to architecting high-performing and cost-efficient data platforms.

This section offers a deep dive into the differences, advantages, limitations, and common use cases for Synapse SQL and Spark pools. We will also explore architectural considerations, performance optimization strategies, integration patterns, and best practices for combining both engines in a cohesive analytics solution.

## Overview of Compute Engines

### Synapse SQL Pools

Synapse SQL offers two modes:

1. **Dedicated SQL Pools (formerly SQL Data Warehouse):**

   ◦ Pre-provisioned, always-on compute resources.

○ Suited for structured data, star/snowflake schemas, and enterprise data warehousing.

2. **Serverless SQL Pools:**

○ On-demand compute for querying files in data lakes.

○ Pay-per-query model.

○ Ideal for ad-hoc exploration of unstructured/ semi-structured data.

**Apache Spark Pools**

Spark pools in Synapse are based on Apache Spark and support distributed data processing. They provide an interactive experience for large-scale data engineering, machine learning, and data science workflows.

**Supported Languages:**

- PySpark
- Scala
- Spark SQL
- .NET for Spark

---

## Core Differences Between SQL and Spark Pools

| Feature | Synapse SQL (Serverless/ Dedicated) | Apache Spark Pools |
|---|---|---|
| Data Processing Model | Declarative (T-SQL) | Programmatic (Spark APIs) |
| Data Types Supported | Structured | Structured, Semi-structured, Unstructured |
| Performance Model | Row-based (Dedicated) or lazy scan (Serverless) | In-memory distributed compute |
| Use Case | BI, reporting, dimensional modeling | ETL, machine learning, big data |
| File Format Support | CSV, Parquet, JSON (via OPENROWSET) | All major formats (including binary) |
| Runtime | Tightly managed | Customizable clusters |
| Integration | Power BI, SQL tooling | ML libraries, notebooks |
| Cost Model | Pay-per-query (Serverless) / Fixed (Dedicated) | Pay-per-job or per-session |

## Use Cases for Synapse SQL

### 1. Data Exploration (Serverless SQL)

Ideal for quickly scanning data in ADLS Gen2 without provisioning infrastructure.

**Example: Querying Parquet File**

SELECT region, COUNT(*) AS order_count

FROM OPENROWSET(

```
BULK 'https://datalake.dfs.core.windows.net/curated/
sales/*.parquet',
FORMAT='PARQUET'
) AS orders
GROUP BY region;
```

**2. Enterprise Data Warehousing (Dedicated SQL)**

- Dimensional modeling (star/snowflake schemas)
- Power BI and reporting integration
- Predictable workloads with optimized performance

**Optimizations:**

- Partitioning by date
- Distribution by hash key
- Materialized views for common aggregates

**3. Real-Time Dashboard Backends**

Use serverless SQL as the backend for Power BI dashboards.

**Advantages:**

- Low latency
- No always-on compute
- Simple integration via Synapse SQL endpoint

## Use Cases for Apache Spark Pools

### 1. ETL and Data Transformation

Apache Spark excels at reading massive files, applying transformations, and writing to lakehouse storage in optimized formats.

**Example: Transform and Write**

```
df = spark.read.parquet("abfss://raw@datalake.dfs.core.windows.net/sales/")

df = df.withColumn("AmountUSD", df["Amount"] * 1.25)

df.write.parquet("abfss://curated@datalake.dfs.core.windows.net/sales_enriched/")
```

### 2. Machine Learning and Feature Engineering

Spark's MLlib and compatibility with libraries like XGBoost, scikit-learn, and SynapseML make it ideal for:

- Feature preparation
- Model training and evaluation
- Scoring large datasets in batch mode

### 3. Streaming and Time-Series Processing

Use Spark Structured Streaming to process data from Event Hubs or IoT Hub in real time and write to ADLS or Synapse tables.

**Streaming Pipeline Example:**

- Ingest telemetry from IoT devices.
- Filter and enrich with reference data.
- Store clean data in lake and serve dashboards.

---

## When to Use Synapse SQL vs Spark

| Scenario | Recommended Engine |
|---|---|
| Simple SQL-based data exploration | Synapse Serverless SQL |
| Building a BI warehouse with Power BI | Synapse Dedicated SQL |
| Ad-hoc analysis on lake files | Serverless SQL |
| Transforming large semi-structured files | Spark |
| Building and deploying ML pipelines | Spark |
| Real-time ingestion and processing | Spark |
| Automating pipeline transformations | Both (SQL for logic, Spark for scale) |

## Combining SQL and Spark in Synapse

One of the most powerful capabilities of Synapse is the **seamless interoperability** between Spark and SQL.

### Shared Metadata

- Databases and tables created in Spark can be accessed via SQL pools, and vice versa.
- Allows mixed-mode workflows (ETL in Spark, reporting in SQL).

**Spark Table Creation:**

```
df.write.saveAsTable("sales_summary")
```

**Query via Serverless SQL:**

```
SELECT * FROM sales_summary WHERE Region = 'EMEA';
```

## Performance Considerations

### SQL Pools

- Use **partitioned and distributed tables** for large fact tables.
- **Use columnstore indexes** for compression and speed.
- **Avoid row-by-row operations**, favor set-based logic.

### Spark Pools

- **Use caching** for repeated data access (df.cache()).

• **Repartition wisely** to balance parallelism and avoid data skew.

• Monitor **stage duration and shuffle size** in Spark UI.

---

## Cost Optimization

### Synapse SQL

• Use **serverless SQL** for intermittent or exploratory work.

• Scale **dedicated pools** based on peak vs. off-peak usage (DWU scale).

```
az synapse sql pool update \
—name salesdw \
—workspace-name synapseworkspace \
—performance-level DW200c
```

### Apache Spark

• Use **autoscale** and **on-demand sessions**.

• Prefer **batch jobs** over long-running sessions.

• Clear cached data after job completion.

```
spark.catalog.clearCache()
```

---

## Development and Tooling

Both SQL and Spark pools integrate with Synapse Studio, enabling:

- Notebooks (Spark)
- SQL Scripts (SQL pools)
- Pipelines (orchestrate both engines)
- Git integration for versioning

Power users can also use:

- **Azure Data Studio** for SQL
- **VS Code** with Jupyter Notebooks for Spark

---

## Real-World Example: Unified Pipeline

**Goal:** Clean sales data, join with region info, summarize, and visualize.

1. Ingest raw CSV with Spark and apply schema.
2. Write Parquet to curated zone.
3. Define external table in serverless SQL.
4. Run summary query for dashboard.

**Benefits:**

- Scale of Spark for transformation
- Familiar SQL interface for analytics
- Efficient storage in lakehouse format

## Summary

Azure Synapse Analytics delivers an exceptional advantage by offering both SQL and Spark compute engines under one platform. Understanding their differences—and more importantly, how they complement each other—is critical for building efficient, scalable, and cost-effective analytics solutions.

Use Synapse SQL for structured data exploration, reporting, and warehousing. Use Apache Spark for complex transformations, machine learning, and processing semi-structured or unstructured data. And when combined effectively, these engines enable a robust, end-to-end lakehouse architecture that powers modern data strategies.

In the next section, we'll explore **Synapse Pipelines and Integration Runtime**, learning how to build, monitor, and orchestrate data workflows using built-in tools and connectors.

# Synapse Pipelines and Integration Runtime

Azure Synapse Pipelines offer a powerful, integrated orchestration engine within Synapse Analytics that enables the creation, monitoring, and management of end-to-end data workflows. Built on the same engine as Azure Data Factory, Synapse Pipelines allow users to move, transform, and load data across various sources and destinations using a visual, code-free interface or through JSON-based configurations for advanced scenarios.

This section explores the capabilities of Synapse Pipelines, including pipeline authoring, data movement, transformation activities, parameterization, triggers, and the role of Integration Runtime (IR).

It provides comprehensive guidance on how to design robust, reusable, and secure data workflows in Azure Synapse Analytics.

## Core Concepts of Synapse Pipelines

A pipeline in Synapse is a logical grouping of activities that together perform a task. Activities can execute data movement, transformations, external executions, and control logic.

**Key Components:**

- **Pipeline**: A container of activities.
- **Activity**: The step that performs a specific operation.
- **Dataset**: Defines schema and metadata pointing to data.
- **Linked Service**: Defines a connection to a data source.
- **Integration Runtime (IR)**: The compute infrastructure used for execution.
- **Trigger**: Defines when a pipeline runs (scheduled, tumbling window, or event-based).
- **Parameters**: Input values for flexible pipeline execution.

## Types of Activities

### 1. Data Movement Activities

Enable copying data from a source to a sink with optional transformations.

**Example:** Moving data from SQL to ADLS Gen2.

```
{
"type": "Copy",
"inputs": [{"name": "SqlDataset"}],
"outputs": [{"name": "AdlsDataset"}],
"typeProperties": {
"source": {"type": "SqlSource"},
"sink": {"type": "ParquetSink"}
}
}
```

### 2. Data Transformation Activities

- **Mapping Data Flows**: Visual data transformation using Spark behind the scenes.
- **Notebook**: Execute Apache Spark code.
- **Stored Procedure**: Call stored procedures in Synapse SQL pools.

**3. Control Flow Activities**

Used for orchestration and logic branching:

- **If Condition**
- **Switch**
- **ForEach**
- **Until**
- **Wait**
- **Set Variable**
- **Execute Pipeline**

**4. External Activities**

- **Web**: Call external REST endpoints.
- **Azure Function**: Trigger Azure Functions for custom logic.
- **Batch Service**: Run batch jobs on external compute.

---

## Authoring Pipelines in Synapse Studio

Synapse Studio provides a no-code/low-code environment to build pipelines:

1. Navigate to the **Integrate** hub.
2. Click + > **Pipeline** to create a new pipeline.

3. Drag and drop activities from the toolbox.
4. Define inputs/outputs and configure parameters.
5. Test and debug using the built-in **Debug** button.
6. Trigger manually or publish for scheduled runs.

Pipelines can also be exported to and maintained via **Azure DevOps or GitHub**, enabling CI/CD workflows.

## Using Integration Runtimes (IR)

Integration Runtime is the compute engine that runs pipeline activities.

**Types of IR:**

| Type | Description |
|---|---|
| AutoResolve IR | Default IR managed by Synapse. Used for most native operations. |
| Azure IR | Used for cloud-based data movement and transformation. |
| Self-hosted IR | Required to connect to on-premises or private networks. |

**Setting Up Self-hosted IR:**

1. Download the IR installer on the on-premises server.
2. Register the IR in Synapse Studio.
3. Use for secure data integration from private networks.

**Monitoring IR Usage:**

Use the **Manage** hub in Synapse Studio to view IR metrics, active jobs, and throughput statistics.

## Data Movement Scenarios

### SQL to ADLS Gen2 (ETL)

- Source: Azure SQL Database
- Sink: Parquet files in ADLS Gen2
- Transformation: Optional Mapping Data Flow

### Blob to Synapse Table (ELT)

- Copy CSV from Blob
- Use PolyBase to load into Dedicated SQL Pool
- Trigger Stored Procedure to transform

**Copy Activity JSON Snippet:**

```
{
"name": "CopyBlobToSynapse",
"type": "Copy",
"inputs": [{"name": "BlobDataset"}],
"outputs": [{"name": "SynapseDataset"}],
"typeProperties": {
"source": {"type": "DelimitedTextSource"},
"sink": {
"type": "SqlSink",
```

```
"writeBatchSize": 10000,

"writeBatchTimeout": "00:05:00"

}

}

}
```

## Pipeline Parameterization

Parameters make pipelines dynamic and reusable. Define them at the pipeline level and pass values during execution.

**Example:**

```
"parameters": {

"sourcePath": {

"type": "string"

},

"targetTable": {

"type": "string"

}

}
```

Use expressions like:

```
@concat('abfss://raw@datalake.dfs.core.windows.net/', pipeline().parameters.sourcePath)
```

## Triggers

Triggers determine **when** and **how often** a pipeline executes.

**Types of Triggers:**

1. **Schedule Trigger**: Runs at specified intervals.
2. **Tumbling Window Trigger**: Fixed-size, non-overlapping intervals. Supports state and retries.
3. **Event-Based Trigger**: Responds to events (e.g., new file in Blob storage).

**Creating a Trigger (Schedule):**

```
{
"type": "ScheduleTrigger",
"typeProperties": {
"recurrence": {
"frequency": "Day",
"interval": 1,
"startTime": "2025-01-01T00:00:00Z"
}
}
}
```

## Monitoring and Alerts

The **Monitor** hub in Synapse Studio provides insights into pipeline execution:

- Pipeline run history
- Success/failure counts
- Duration of each activity
- Triggered runs and parameters used

You can configure alerts using **Azure Monitor** for:

- Failed activities
- Long-running jobs
- Execution anomalies

**Example KQL for Failed Pipelines:**

```
SynapsePipelineRuns
| where Status == "Failed"
| summarize count() by PipelineName, bin(TimeGenerated, 1h)
```

## Best Practices for Synapse Pipelines

1. **Use parameterization** for reusable and modular pipelines.
2. **Use lookup and ForEach** for dynamically generating tasks.
3. **Modularize logic** by creating sub-pipelines and invoking via Execute Pipeline activity.
4. **Enable retry policies** for transient errors (e.g., network

timeouts).

5. **Implement logging** into a dedicated monitoring table or log analytics workspace.
6. **Version control** pipelines with Git integration.

---

## Example Use Case: Daily Ingestion and Transformation

**Objective:** Load sales data every night from an FTP source, clean it, and load it into a reporting table.

**Pipeline Steps:**

1. **Web Activity**: Call API to fetch metadata.
2. **Copy Activity**: Download files from FTP (via self-hosted IR).
3. **Data Flow Activity**: Remove nulls, standardize formats.
4. **Stored Procedure Activity**: Update summary tables in SQL pool.
5. **If Condition**: Send alert if row count < threshold.

**Trigger:** Scheduled daily at midnight.

**Monitoring:** Azure Monitor sends email if Copy Activity duration > 15 minutes.

---

## Summary

Synapse Pipelines are the orchestration engine at the heart of data integration in Synapse Analytics. They provide the tools necessary to automate data movement, execute complex transformation logic, and manage data flows from ingestion to presentation. Whether you're designing batch ETL pipelines, real-time data workflows, or parameterized templates for large-scale integration, Synapse Pipelines provide the flexibility, scalability, and reliability required in modern data platforms.

The Integration Runtime serves as the backbone for compute and connectivity, enabling secure, distributed execution across cloud and hybrid environments. Together, these tools allow data engineers to build robust, maintainable, and production-ready pipelines for every analytics scenario.

In the next chapter, we'll explore **Real-Time Analytics and Streaming Data**, where services like Azure Stream Analytics and Event Hubs enable processing and visualizing data with near-zero latency.

# Chapter 5: Data Movement and Integration with Azure Data Factory

## ETL vs ELT Paradigms in Azure

Data movement and transformation are foundational components of any data platform. In modern cloud architectures, these processes are typically implemented using two dominant paradigms: **ETL (Extract, Transform, Load)** and **ELT (Extract, Load, Transform)**. Azure Data Factory (ADF), Azure Synapse Analytics, and other services in the Azure ecosystem support both approaches, but selecting the right one depends on data volume, latency requirements, data source variety, and system architecture.

In this section, we'll explore ETL and ELT in depth, comparing their advantages, ideal use cases, implementation patterns in Azure, and how Azure Data Factory enables organizations to build scalable, efficient, and maintainable data pipelines using either or both paradigms.

---

### Understanding ETL and ELT

#### ETL: Extract, Transform, Load

ETL is the traditional approach used in on-premises environments and early data warehouse architectures.

1. **Extract** – Retrieve data from source systems (databases, APIs, files).
2. **Transform** – Clean, filter, join, and aggregate data in a staging environment (outside the target database).
3. **Load** – Insert the transformed data into the destination

(data warehouse or data lake).

**Typical ETL Tools:** SSIS, Informatica, Talend, and Azure Data Factory with Mapping Data Flows.

**Key Features:**

- Transformation occurs outside of the data warehouse.
- Often implemented using Spark or other data engines.
- Suitable for strict governance and controlled pipelines.

**ELT: Extract, Load, Transform**

ELT is better suited for cloud-scale data platforms, leveraging the power of the data warehouse or lakehouse for transformation.

1. **Extract** – Data is pulled from source systems.
2. **Load** – Raw data is ingested directly into the data lake or warehouse.
3. **Transform** – Data is cleaned and transformed **within** the target system using SQL or Spark.

**Typical ELT Tools:** Azure Synapse Pipelines, T-SQL scripts, dbt, stored procedures.

**Key Features:**

- Exploits MPP (Massively Parallel Processing) capabilities.
- Better performance for large datasets.

- Keeps raw data accessible for future transformations or reprocessing.

---

## Comparison of ETL vs ELT

| Feature | ETL | ELT |
|---|---|---|
| Transformation Location | Outside the destination (in engine or tool) | Inside the destination (SQL/Spark) |
| Performance | Limited by external compute | Uses warehouse compute (e.g., Synapse) |
| Data Volume | Moderate to high | High to massive |
| Raw Data Preservation | Not always retained | Usually retained |
| Tools in Azure | ADF Mapping Data Flows, Data Bricks | Synapse SQL, Serverless SQL, Spark Pools |
| Use Case | Compliance, curated transformations | Data exploration, modern analytics |

## ETL Implementation in Azure

In Azure, the ETL approach can be implemented using:

- **Azure Data Factory + Mapping Data Flows**
- **Azure Databricks**
- **Azure Synapse Pipelines + Notebooks**

### ETL with ADF Mapping Data Flows

Mapping Data Flows in ADF offer a code-free design experience backed by Spark execution.

**Example Scenario:**

- Extract customer data from SQL Server.
- Join with product data from Blob Storage.
- Apply currency conversion and null handling.
- Load to curated zone in ADLS Gen2.

**Advantages:**

- Visual interface.
- Built-in transformations (filter, join, pivot, aggregate).
- Auto-scaling via Azure IR.

**Pipeline Steps:**

1. Define Linked Services for source and sink.
2. Create datasets (e.g., customer.csv).
3. Design data flow with transformation logic.
4. Execute pipeline with scheduled trigger.

---

## ELT Implementation in Azure

In Azure, ELT is often the preferred choice due to Synapse Analytics' ability to handle large transformations efficiently.

### ELT Using Synapse SQL

**Workflow:**

1. Use ADF Copy Activity to load raw data into a staging table.
2. Run stored procedures or SQL scripts to transform data.
3. Output final results to reporting tables or Power BI datasets.

**Benefits:**

- Leverages dedicated SQL pool compute.
- Simpler logic using T-SQL.
- More traceable and modular.

**Sample T-SQL Transformation:**

```
INSERT INTO sales_cleaned (OrderID, CustomerID, AmountUSD)

SELECT OrderID, CustomerID, Amount * 1.12

FROM sales_raw

WHERE OrderDate >= '2024-01-01';
```

**ELT Using Serverless SQL Pools**

Serverless SQL is suitable for querying and transforming Parquet or CSV files directly from ADLS Gen2.

**Example:**

```
SELECT region, SUM(amount) AS total_sales

FROM OPENROWSET(
```

BULK 'https://datalake.dfs.core.windows.net/raw/sales/2024/*.parquet',

FORMAT = 'PARQUET'

) AS sales

GROUP BY region;

Results can be visualized directly in Power BI or exported via pipelines.

---

## Hybrid ETL/ELT Patterns

Many organizations implement a **hybrid approach**, leveraging both paradigms based on the nature of data and the maturity of their platform.

**Example:**

- Use ETL for heavily validated, governed data (e.g., financials).
- Use ELT for raw ingestion, ad-hoc exploration, and data science pipelines.

**Pattern 1: Raw Ingestion → Curated via Spark → Load to SQL**

1. Copy raw CSV to ADLS.
2. Clean and join in Spark pool.
3. Load result into Synapse Dedicated SQL.

**Pattern 2: Copy to SQL Staging → Transform in SQL → Push to BI**

1. Use ADF Copy Activity to push from SAP to SQL staging table.
2. Use T-SQL transformations and store procedure.
3. Publish to reporting views.

---

## Parameterization and Dynamic Pipelines

Both ETL and ELT pipelines benefit from parameterization:

- Source path or file name
- Load date or watermark
- Target schema/table

**Example Expression:**

@concat('sales/year=', formatDateTime(pipeline().parameters.loadDate, 'yyyy'), '/')

Pipelines can be reused across environments (dev, test, prod) by using dynamic parameters.

---

## Monitoring and Debugging

Whether using ETL or ELT, pipeline monitoring is critical for reliability.

**ADF Monitoring Features:**

- Activity logs per run

- Retry policies
- Failure alerts via Azure Monitor
- Integration with Log Analytics

**Best Practice:** Log row counts, timestamps, and error messages into an audit table or storage log for traceability.

---

## Security Considerations

- Use **Managed Identity** for all services.
- Restrict access via **RBAC** and **Network Rules**.
- Mask sensitive data at source or during transformation.
- Encrypt all transit paths using HTTPS and private endpoints.

---

## Best Practices

1. **Choose ELT when possible** for performance and flexibility.
2. **Use Mapping Data Flows** for complex transformations requiring a visual interface.
3. **Partition and compress** files during load to minimize scan cost.
4. **Track lineage** using Azure Purview or a metadata table.
5. **Build modular pipelines** with error handling and reusability in mind.
6. **Validate data** before and after transformations.

---

## Summary

Understanding the distinctions between ETL and ELT is crucial for building scalable and maintainable data platforms on Azure. ETL remains important for regulated, structured pipelines, especially when external transformation engines are required. ELT, however, is the modern standard in cloud-first analytics architectures due to its scalability, performance, and ease of maintenance.

With Azure Data Factory, Synapse Analytics, and supporting services, architects can design dynamic, resilient workflows that fit their data maturity level and business goals. Whether implementing ELT for fast-moving IoT streams or traditional ETL for financial compliance, Azure's tools provide the flexibility and power to meet the challenge.

In the next section, we'll explore how to **build and monitor pipelines** using Azure Data Factory's full feature set, diving into authoring tools, activities, linked services, and monitoring dashboards.

# Building and Monitoring Pipelines

Azure Data Factory (ADF) is Azure's cloud-based data integration service that allows you to create, schedule, and orchestrate data workflows at scale. In Synapse Analytics, this same orchestration engine is embedded within Synapse Pipelines. Whether you're moving terabytes of data from an on-premises SQL Server to Azure Data Lake Storage Gen2 or transforming JSON logs into curated Parquet tables, building and monitoring pipelines is central to delivering reliable data flows.

This section will guide you through the essential processes of building robust data pipelines, configuring and deploying them, and monitoring execution for performance, reliability, and compliance. You'll also learn about reusable patterns, error handling, scheduling, and integration with external services for alerts and audit trails.

---

## Creating Pipelines in Azure Data Factory and Synapse

Pipelines in ADF and Synapse are created in a graphical UI within the Azure portal or Synapse Studio.

**Steps to Create a Pipeline:**

1. **Navigate to the Integrate Hub** in Synapse Studio or the Author section in ADF.
2. Click on **New Pipeline**.
3. Drag and drop activities from the toolbox (e.g., Copy Data, Data Flow).
4. Define **Linked Services** to connect to data sources and destinations.
5. Add **Datasets** to represent tables or files.
6. Configure **activity settings** and **parameters**.
7. Validate and **debug** before publishing.

---

## Core Pipeline Components

### 1. Linked Services

Linked Services define the connection strings and credentials to data sources like Azure SQL, ADLS, Blob Storage, REST APIs, etc.

```
{
"name": "AzureDataLakeStorage1",
```

```
"type": "LinkedService",
"typeProperties": {
"url": "https://mydatalake.dfs.core.windows.net",
"authentication": "MSI"
}
}
```

**2. Datasets**

A dataset represents a specific data structure—like a file, folder, or database table—within a linked service.

Example: A CSV file stored in a folder within ADLS Gen2.

**3. Activities**

Activities are the building blocks of a pipeline. Each activity performs a specific task.

**Common Activities:**

- **Copy Data**: Move data between source and sink.
- **Data Flow**: Transform data using Spark-powered UI logic.
- **Execute Pipeline**: Invoke another pipeline.
- **If Condition / Switch**: Control logic.
- **Web / Azure Function**: Call external services.

### 4. Parameters and Variables

Used to make pipelines dynamic and reusable. Pass values like file names, dates, or connection strings.

**Parameter Example:**

"parameters": {

"targetFolder": {

"type": "String"

}

}

Use in expression:

"@concat('curated/', pipeline().parameters.targetFolder, '/')"

### 5. Triggers

Triggers define when a pipeline should execute:

- **Schedule**: Run on a time interval.
- **Tumbling Window**: Fixed-size intervals.
- **Event**: Based on blob events or custom event grid messages.
- **Manual**: Triggered on demand.

---

## Building Common Patterns

### Pattern 1: Ingest from SQL to Data Lake

1. Copy data from Azure SQL to ADLS Gen2.
2. Parameterize schema and table name.
3. Store in a dated folder structure (e.g., /raw/sales/2025/04/01/).

### Pattern 2: Ingest and Transform

1. Use Copy Activity to ingest raw data.
2. Use Mapping Data Flow to clean, filter, and enrich.
3. Output to curated zone with Parquet format.

### Pattern 3: Loop Over Multiple Sources

1. Use Lookup activity to read metadata (e.g., source tables).
2. Use ForEach to loop over rows and trigger ingestion for each.

```
{
"name": "ForEachTable",
"type": "ForEach",
"items": "@activity('LookupTables').output.value",
"activities": [
{
"name": "CopyTable",
```

```
"type": "Copy",
"inputs": [{"name": "DynamicSource"}],
"outputs": [{"name": "DynamicSink"}]
}
]
}
```

## Debugging and Validation

Before publishing, always use the **Debug** feature to:

- Validate dataset connectivity.
- Inspect parameter values.
- Review transformation logic in Mapping Data Flows.

Mapping Data Flows include a **Data Preview** feature that allows you to see intermediate results after each transformation step.

## Monitoring Pipelines

Synapse and ADF provide integrated monitoring dashboards to review execution history.

**Monitor Capabilities:**

- View pipeline runs and activity status.
- Inspect duration, input/output row counts.
- Filter by status: Succeeded, Failed, Cancelled.

- Access error messages and retry failed activities.

**Accessing Logs:**

1. Use the **Monitor Hub** in Synapse Studio or ADF.
2. Drill into pipeline details to see activity run times.
3. Export logs to **Log Analytics** for advanced analysis.

**Sample KQL Query in Log Analytics:**

```
ADFActivityRun

| where Status == "Failed"

| summarize count() by ActivityName, ResourceId, bin(TimeGenerated, 1h)
```

---

## Alerts and Notifications

To stay ahead of issues, configure alerts for pipeline failures or slow runs.

**Integration Options:**

- Azure Monitor Alerts
- Action Groups (Email, SMS, Webhooks)
- Logic Apps (send Teams or Slack alerts)

**Example: Alert on pipeline failure:**

1. Create metric alert on PipelineRunsFailed.
2. Trigger Logic App to send a custom email.

---

## Error Handling and Recovery

Use built-in features to make pipelines fault-tolerant:

- **Retry policies**: Set max retries and intervals for transient issues.
- **Timeouts**: Prevent hanging executions.
- **Custom logging**: Insert metadata into an audit table or blob storage.
- **Failure branches**: Use IfCondition or OnFailure paths for remediation.

**Example Recovery Logic:**

- On failure of Copy Activity, invoke Web Activity to notify an admin.
- Log error to a storage file with timestamp and failure message.

---

## Best Practices

1. **Use modular pipelines** – Break large workflows into reusable components.
2. **Centralize parameter configuration** – Use global config files or control tables.
3. **Automate deployment** – Integrate ADF with Azure DevOps or GitHub Actions.
4. **Secure linked services** – Prefer managed identity or Key Vault secrets.
5. **Use naming conventions** – For pipelines, datasets, triggers,

and folders.

6. **Track lineage** – Store input/output metadata for each activity.

---

## CI/CD and Version Control

Pipelines should be version-controlled and part of your CI/CD workflows.

- Use **Git integration** (Azure DevOps or GitHub).
- Separate branches for dev/test/prod environments.
- Automate deployment using ARM templates or ADF Tools for Azure DevOps.

**CI/CD Flow:**

1. Commit JSON pipeline definitions to Git.
2. Run validation checks and publish artifacts.
3. Deploy to target environment via release pipelines.

---

## Summary

Building and monitoring pipelines in Azure Data Factory or Synapse Analytics enables organizations to create enterprise-grade data workflows that are reliable, reusable, and scalable. From basic copy operations to complex transformations involving branching logic, parameterization, and parallel execution, Synapse Pipelines offer a rich set of capabilities for orchestrating data integration across cloud and hybrid systems.

Monitoring and alerting are just as important as pipeline logic—ensuring operational stability, observability, and compliance. By following best practices and using the built-in tools for versioning, security, and modular design, teams can streamline the development and management of data pipelines that form the backbone of their analytics ecosystem.

In the next section, we'll explore **Data Flows and Mapping Data** in greater depth, including how to visually build transformations that scale using Spark under the hood.

# Data Flows and Mapping Data

Mapping Data Flows in Azure Data Factory (ADF) and Synapse Pipelines provide a code-free, visual interface to design and implement complex data transformation logic. They are built on top of Azure Databricks and use Apache Spark as their execution engine, enabling scalable, distributed processing for high-volume data transformation tasks.

Mapping Data Flows bridge the gap between traditional ETL tools and modern big data processing by allowing data engineers to build powerful transformation logic without writing a single line of code—though expressions and dynamic content can be embedded as needed. This section covers everything from the fundamentals of Mapping Data Flows, to transformation functions, performance tuning, and real-world use cases.

## What Are Mapping Data Flows?

A Mapping Data Flow is a visually designed data transformation logic that executes on a Spark cluster managed by ADF or Synapse. It allows you to ingest, clean, transform, join, and output data using a graphical user interface that can run in batch or trigger-based pipelines.

**Key Features:**

- Built-in support for multiple data sources (ADLS, Blob, SQL, REST, etc.).
- Executed via **Data Flow Activity** in pipelines.
- Automatic scale-out and memory management.
- Native support for row-level and column-level transformations.
- Output formats include Parquet, CSV, JSON, Delta Lake, and others.

---

## When to Use Mapping Data Flows

Use Mapping Data Flows when:

- You need to apply multi-step transformations without hand-coding.
- You need to perform data wrangling at scale.
- You're working with large files in ADLS Gen2 or Blob storage.
- You require parallelism and distributed compute for performance.

Avoid if:

- You have small datasets (use Copy Activity with SQL expressions).
- You require low-latency processing (use Azure Functions or Stream Analytics).

---

## Anatomy of a Data Flow

A typical Data Flow includes the following components:

1. **Source** – Defines the input dataset.
2. **Transformations** – One or more transformations applied to the data.
3. **Sink** – The destination dataset to which results are written.
4. **Settings** – Optimizations like partitioning, cache, broadcast joins, and debug mode.

**Example Flow:**

SQL Source → Filter Nulls → Join with Lookup Table → Aggregate → Parquet Sink

---

## Common Transformation Types

### 1. Select

Choose specific columns, rename them, or change their data types.

### 2. Filter

Apply conditional logic to exclude or include rows.

isNull(OrderDate) == false && Amount > 0

**3. Derived Column**

Create new columns using expressions or modify existing ones.

AmountUSD = Amount * 1.25

**4. Conditional Split**

Route rows to different streams based on conditions.

Amount > 1000 → "HighValue"

Amount <= 1000 → "Standard"

**5. Aggregate**

Group data by columns and apply aggregations like sum, count, average.

groupBy: [Region]

aggregates: sum(Amount), count(OrderID)

**6. Join**

Combine rows from two datasets using inner, left, right, or outer joins.

Join Condition: source.CustomerID == lookup.CustomerID

**7. Pivot / Unpivot**

Transform rows into columns and vice versa.

#### 8. Surrogate Key

Add auto-incrementing or hash-based keys.

#### 9. Exists

Check for the presence of records in another dataset (similar to SQL EXISTS).

---

## Expressions and Functions

Data Flows use a powerful expression language similar to SQL and functional languages like Scala.

**Examples:**

- toTimestamp(OrderDate, 'MM/dd/yyyy')
- iif(Amount > 5000, 'VIP', 'Regular')
- concat(firstName, ' ', lastName)
- round(Amount, 2)

Functions are grouped into categories:

- **DateTime**: now(), toDate(), addDays()
- **String**: upper(), substring(), replace()
- **Math**: round(), ceil(), floor()
- **Array/Object**: collect(), byName()

---

## Source and Sink Configuration

**Source Options:**

- SQL Database
- Azure Blob Storage
- ADLS Gen2
- REST API
- Cosmos DB
- Amazon S3 (via linked service)

You can configure:

- Projection (schema inference)
- Schema drift (handling columns not defined in schema)
- Partitioning for parallel read

**Sink Options:**

- ADLS Gen2 (Parquet, CSV, JSON)
- Azure SQL Database
- Azure Synapse Analytics
- Azure Cosmos DB
- Blob Storage

Sink settings include:

- File naming options
- Truncate table before load
- Insert vs upsert
- Row-level upserts via keys

---

## Debugging and Testing

ADF and Synapse provide a **Data Flow Debug** feature that launches a Spark cluster for interactive testing.

**Features:**

- View row-level preview after each transformation.
- Inspect data types and column values.
- Test expression logic interactively.
- Limit rows to reduce cluster costs.

**Tip:** Use sample files or small partitions for debugging. Always disable debug mode in production pipelines.

---

## Performance Optimization

To improve the efficiency of Mapping Data Flows:

**1. Optimize Join Strategy**

- Use broadcast join if one side is small.
- Hash partition large datasets on join keys.

**2. Use Caching**

For datasets reused multiple times within a flow.

Enable Cache = true

**3. Partitioning**

Control how data is distributed across Spark executors.

- **Round Robin**: General use, even distribution.
- **Hash**: On specific column for joins or aggregations.
- **Single Partition**: Useful for small datasets.

**4. Set Sink Batch Size**

Reduce file size or batch load pressure on target systems.

**5. Disable Schema Drift**

If the schema is known and stable, turn off schema drift to improve performance.

## Error Handling in Data Flows

Use error row handling settings at the **source**, **sink**, or **individual transformations**:

- **Skip rows on error**: Ignore and log problematic rows.
- **Redirect rows**: Send bad rows to another output stream.
- **Fail on error**: Stop execution immediately (default behavior).

You can also configure error policies at the Sink level:

"errorRowHandling": "Redirect"

---

## Real-World Use Cases

### Case 1: ETL for Retail Analytics

- Source: Azure SQL Database
- Transform: Clean nulls, join with product metadata, apply currency conversions
- Sink: Curated zone in Parquet format for Power BI

### Case 2: Health Data Cleansing

- Source: JSON logs from ADLS Gen2
- Transform: Parse nested fields, remove outliers, hash patient IDs

- Sink: HIPAA-compliant SQL database

**Case 3: Multi-Region Aggregation**

- Source: CSV files from different regions
- Transform: Normalize schemas, convert timezones, unify currencies
- Sink: Partitioned Parquet files in Synapse-linked storage

---

## Deployment and Lifecycle

Mapping Data Flows can be deployed via:

- Azure DevOps (ARM templates or JSON files)
- GitHub Actions
- Azure CLI and REST API
- Synapse or ADF Studio publish buttons

**Versioning Tip:** Use Git branches to manage feature additions, and validate changes in test environments before promoting.

---

## Summary

Mapping Data Flows provide a scalable, visual, and code-free way to design data transformations in Azure. With their native support for Spark-based execution, they handle high-volume workloads efficiently while offering rich transformation capabilities. Whether you're shaping data for a business dashboard, preparing features for machine learning, or normalizing complex file formats, Mapping Data Flows reduce development time and increase maintainability.

In the next section, we'll explore how to work with on-premises and cloud-based data sources simultaneously, including hybrid integration scenarios, Self-hosted Integration Runtime setup, and secure data movement between environments.

## Working with On-Prem and Cloud Sources

In a typical enterprise environment, data exists across a spectrum of locations—ranging from legacy on-premises systems to modern cloud-native platforms. Integrating these data sources is a critical task for any data engineer or architect aiming to build a unified analytics pipeline. Azure Data Factory (ADF) and Synapse Pipelines provide robust capabilities to connect, ingest, transform, and move data between on-prem and cloud environments securely and efficiently.

This section focuses on how to enable hybrid data integration scenarios, configure Self-hosted Integration Runtime (SHIR), establish secure connections, implement pipelines for hybrid data movement, and follow best practices to maintain high performance, reliability, and compliance in such architectures.

---

### Challenges in Hybrid Data Integration

Hybrid data environments present unique challenges that cloud-native solutions don't typically face:

- Network connectivity across firewalls and proxies
- Authentication across multiple identity systems

- Latency and performance variability
- Data sovereignty and regulatory concerns
- Legacy formats and systems

ADF and Synapse Pipelines bridge these gaps through their hybrid connectivity model, built around **Self-hosted Integration Runtime** and secure linking of on-prem and cloud assets.

## Integration Runtime Types

Before diving into hybrid scenarios, it's essential to understand the types of Integration Runtime (IR) and their use cases.

| IR Type | Description |
|---|---|
| Azure IR | Managed by Microsoft, used for cloud-to-cloud data movement |
| Self-hosted IR (SHIR) | Installed on-prem or VM to connect to private networks |
| AutoResolve IR | Synapse's default managed IR for linked services in the same region |

## Setting Up Self-Hosted Integration Runtime

SHIR allows ADF or Synapse Pipelines to securely access on-prem systems behind a firewall or inside a private network.

### Step-by-Step Installation

1. Go to **Manage > Integration Runtimes** in Synapse Studio or ADF.
2. Click **New** and choose **Self-Hosted**.
3. Provide a name and description.

4. Click **Download and install the integration runtime.**
5. Install it on a machine that has access to your on-prem systems (Windows Server recommended).
6. Register the IR using the auto-generated authentication key.

**System Requirements**

- Windows Server 2012 or later
- Minimum 4 cores, 8 GB RAM
- Outbound port 443 open (for Azure communication)
- Optional: High-availability configuration using a secondary node

**High Availability**

Install the SHIR on two or more machines. During registration, use the same key for both. This creates an HA cluster where pipelines automatically fail over if one node becomes unavailable.

## Connecting to On-Prem Systems

Once SHIR is installed, you can create Linked Services to connect to:

- SQL Server
- Oracle
- SAP

- File systems (SMB shares)
- REST APIs hosted on-prem

**Example: SQL Server Linked Service via SHIR**

```
{
"name": "SqlServerOnPrem",
"type": "LinkedService",
"typeProperties": {
"connectionString": "Server=sqlserver01;Database=ERP;",
"authenticationType": "Windows",
"userName": "domain\\username",
"password": "******"
},
"connectVia": {
"referenceName": "SelfHostedIR01",
"type": "IntegrationRuntimeReference"
}
}
```

## Common On-Prem to Cloud Scenarios

### Scenario 1: Extracting Data from On-Prem SQL to ADLS

- Use Copy Activity to move data from on-prem SQL to ADLS.
- Use Mapping Data Flow or Synapse Spark for transformation.
- Load curated data into Power BI or Synapse SQL for analysis.

### Scenario 2: Syncing Files from Local SMB Share

- Use SHIR to connect to a file system.
- Use wildcard filters to select only new or modified files.
- Compress and encrypt data during upload.

### Scenario 3: Hybrid ETL with On-Prem Source and Cloud Sink

- Extract data using SHIR from Oracle or SAP.
- Transform using Mapping Data Flow or in-database logic.
- Load results into Azure SQL Database or Synapse tables.

## Security Considerations

### Network Security

- No inbound ports required.
- All communication is **outbound** from SHIR to Azure over HTTPS (port 443).
- Uses Azure Relay for connectivity.

### Identity and Access Control

- Prefer **Managed Identity** or Azure Key Vault for storing credentials.
- Use **Azure RBAC** for pipeline access management.
- Encrypt data in transit and at rest.

### Data Masking and Tokenization

For sensitive data, apply transformations before moving to the cloud:

- Use Derived Column in Mapping Data Flows to hash or mask values.
- Encrypt payloads using client-side logic or SHIR custom command hooks.

---

## Monitoring Hybrid Pipelines

Use the **Monitor** hub in Synapse Studio or ADF to view:

- SHIR activity health
- Pipeline execution details
- Throughput metrics and errors

Enable **Diagnostic Settings** to export logs to Azure Log Analytics or Event Hub.

**Sample KQL Query:**

ADFActivityRun

| where Status == "Failed" and LinkedServiceName contains "OnPrem"

| project PipelineName, ActivityName, Error, TimeGenerated

Set up alerts on:

- SHIR offline status
- Failed connections
- Long-running pipeline executions

---

## Performance Optimization Tips

1. **Use batch queries** when pulling large datasets from on-prem databases.
2. **Push filters** to source systems via SQL expressions.
3. **Enable parallelism** by partitioning on ID or date columns.
4. **Compress files** (GZip or Parquet) during transfer to reduce network load.
5. **Schedule jobs** during off-peak hours to minimize resource

contention.

---

## Best Practices for Hybrid Integration

- **Test SHIR connectivity** with test queries before deploying full pipelines.
- **Version control** all pipeline artifacts and integration configurations.
- **Audit** every step of the pipeline for compliance and troubleshooting.
- **Validate data integrity** by logging row counts or checksums before and after transfers.
- **Establish SLA metrics** (e.g., latency, data freshness, recovery time).

---

## Real-World Use Case: Financial Reporting Integration

**Challenge**: A multinational organization maintains its ERP systems on-premises while building its analytics infrastructure in Azure.

**Solution**:

1. Install SHIR on a secure VM in their data center.
2. Extract daily sales and ledger records from SQL Server.
3. Copy data to Azure Data Lake in Parquet format.
4. Transform using Synapse Mapping Data Flows.
5. Publish financial KPIs to Power BI via Synapse SQL views.

**Outcome**:

- Reduced reporting time from 2 days to 4 hours.
- Improved traceability and security compliance.
- Centralized monitoring of all data movement activities.

---

## Summary

Hybrid data integration is a cornerstone of modern enterprise data architecture. With Azure Data Factory and Synapse Pipelines, organizations can securely and efficiently bridge their legacy on-prem systems with cloud-native analytics platforms. By leveraging Self-hosted Integration Runtime, robust pipeline orchestration, and best practices in security and performance, you can ensure reliable, scalable, and compliant data flows across environments.

As we move into the next chapter, we'll explore how real-time analytics and streaming data architectures can be implemented using services like Azure Stream Analytics and Event Hubs—unlocking new use cases such as fraud detection, telemetry processing, and live dashboarding.

# Chapter 6: Real-Time Analytics and Streaming Data

## Azure Stream Analytics Overview

Real-time data analytics is becoming increasingly vital for organizations seeking instant insights from rapidly generated data sources such as IoT devices, financial transactions, logs, and social media feeds. Azure Stream Analytics (ASA) is a fully managed, real-time analytics engine designed to handle this type of data. It enables users to process and analyze streaming data on the fly, with minimal setup and deep integration across the Azure ecosystem.

This section delves into the architecture, capabilities, query model, use cases, and deployment patterns for Azure Stream Analytics. We'll explore how it fits into a broader streaming pipeline and how to integrate it with services like Event Hubs, IoT Hub, Power BI, Synapse, and Azure Data Lake Storage Gen2.

---

### What is Azure Stream Analytics?

Azure Stream Analytics is a real-time data processing engine that ingests streams of data and allows users to write SQL-like queries to filter, aggregate, join, and analyze incoming data. It is scalable, fault-tolerant, and supports integration with various inputs and outputs natively.

**Key Features:**

- **Fully managed**: No infrastructure to maintain.

- **SQL-based query language**: Familiar and simple syntax.

- **Real-time insights**: Millisecond-latency data processing.

- **Windowing functions**: Tumbling, hopping, sliding, session windows.

- **Event ordering and late arrival handling.**

- **Geospatial support**: Analyze data with spatial functions.

- **AI integration**: Built-in support for calling Azure ML models.

---

## ASA Architecture and Components

Azure Stream Analytics applications are built on the following three core components:

1. **Input** – The source of streaming data.
2. **Query** – The logic to process the incoming data.
3. **Output** – Where the processed results are delivered.

**Input Types:**

- **Azure Event Hubs**: Large-scale data ingestion.

- **Azure IoT Hub**: For IoT telemetry.

- **Azure Blob Storage**: Stream historical data or reference data.

- **Azure Data Lake Storage Gen2** (for reference data only).
- **Custom inputs via REST API**.

**Output Types:**

- Azure Data Lake Storage Gen2
- Azure SQL Database / Azure Synapse
- Power BI
- Cosmos DB
- Service Bus / Event Hub
- Blob Storage

---

## Writing Queries in ASA

The ASA query language is a variant of T-SQL, extended with stream processing constructs.

**Example: Basic Filter and Projection**

```
SELECT

DeviceId,

Temperature,

EventEnqueuedUtcTime

FROM
```

IoTInput

WHERE

Temperature > 30

**Windowing: Tumbling Window**

SELECT

COUNT(*) AS EventCount,

System.Timestamp AS WindowEnd

FROM

EventHubInput

GROUP BY

TumblingWindow(minute, 5)

**Windowing: Hopping Window**

SELECT

AVG(Temperature) AS AvgTemp,

System.Timestamp AS WindowEnd

FROM

IoTInput

GROUP BY

HoppingWindow(minute, 10, 5)

**Joining Streams with Reference Data**

```
SELECT
s.DeviceId,
s.Temperature,
d.DeviceLocation
FROM
IoTInput s
JOIN
DeviceReference d
ON
s.DeviceId = d.DeviceId
```

## Integration with Other Azure Services

### Event Hubs

Event Hubs is the recommended ingestion mechanism for high-throughput, real-time data. It is ideal for telemetry, logs, and messaging.

- Automatically partitions data for parallel processing.
- ASA can directly bind to Event Hub as an input source.

**IoT Hub**

Built on top of Event Hubs, IoT Hub provides bi-directional communication with devices.

- Native ASA input type.
- Supports device twin and message routing integration.

**Azure Synapse Analytics**

Stream data can be written directly into Synapse using ASA output. Ideal for real-time dashboards and historical analytics.

**Power BI**

ASA can output real-time dashboards directly to Power BI.

- Enable **Power BI streaming dataset**.
- Configure output in ASA to push to the dashboard.

---

## Handling Late or Out-of-Order Data

ASA supports **event time processing**, meaning you can define how to handle events that arrive late or out of order.

**Example: Late Arrival Tolerance**

```
{
"eventOrderingPolicy": "Adjust",
"lateArrivalTolerance": "00:05:00"
```

```
}
```

Use the System.Timestamp property to reference the actual event time for precise analysis.

## Geospatial Processing

ASA includes support for geospatial functions such as CreatePoint, STDistance, and STWithin.

**Example: Proximity Alert**

```
SELECT

DeviceId,

Location,

ReferencePoint,

STDistance(Location, ReferencePoint) AS Distance

FROM

GeoInput

WHERE

STDistance(Location, ReferencePoint) < 100
```

This is useful for fleet tracking, asset monitoring, and geofencing scenarios.

## Deploying ASA Jobs

**Deployment Methods:**

- **Azure Portal**: Create and configure using UI.
- **Azure CLI**: Automate deployment in CI/CD pipelines.
- **ARM Templates / Bicep**: Infrastructure-as-Code for full reproducibility.
- **Visual Studio Code Extension**: Local development and publishing support.

**Sample CLI Deployment:**

```
az stream-analytics job create \
—name RetailAnalyticsJob \
—resource-group StreamRG \
—location eastus \
—output-error-policy Drop \
—output-start-mode JobStartTime
```

---

## Monitoring and Diagnostics

Monitoring is essential for operational success in stream processing.

**Built-in Monitoring:**

- ASA Portal shows input/output metrics, backpressure alerts, and latency stats.
- Query errors and warnings are logged.
- Integration with **Log Analytics** for advanced telemetry.

**Sample KQL Query in Log Analytics:**

```
AzureDiagnostics
| where ResourceType == "STREAMINGJOBS"
| summarize avg(DurationMs) by bin(TimeGenerated, 5m)
```

**Alerts:**

- Set alerts on metrics like **Input Events, Output Events**, and **Backlogged Events**.
- Route alerts to email, webhooks, or Logic Apps.

---

## Performance Tuning and Scalability

1. **Parallelism**: Configure Streaming Units (SUs) based on input size and transformation complexity.
2. **Partitioning**: Match Event Hub partitions with ASA parallelism.
3. **Optimize Queries**:

- ○ Reduce joins.
- ○ Use filters early.
- ○ Avoid excessive window overlap.

4. **Error Tolerance**: Use retry policies and alternate outputs.

**Note**: ASA scales by increasing Streaming Units (SUs), which add compute and memory resources.

## Use Cases

### 1. Fraud Detection

- Ingest transactions in real-time.
- Apply anomaly detection models via Azure ML.
- Alert on suspicious patterns.

### 2. IoT Telemetry

- Monitor sensor streams from manufacturing or logistics.
- Trigger alerts on threshold breaches.
- Analyze trends in device health.

### 3. Social Media Sentiment

- Analyze tweets or messages in real-time.

- Apply keyword-based filtering.
- Aggregate and visualize trending topics.

**4. Application Monitoring**

- Stream logs from applications.
- Detect spikes in errors or response times.
- Feed to Power BI dashboards or SIEM systems.

---

## Summary

Azure Stream Analytics is a powerful, fully managed service for real-time stream processing. Its SQL-like syntax, deep Azure integration, and ability to process millions of events per second make it ideal for operational intelligence, monitoring, and real-time analytics. By connecting it with Event Hubs, IoT Hub, Synapse, and Power BI, organizations can build dynamic, scalable solutions that respond instantly to new data.

In the next section, we'll explore how to set up **Event Hubs and IoT Integration**, establishing ingestion pipelines from connected devices and external systems to enable seamless streaming into the Azure analytics ecosystem.

# Event Hubs and IoT Integration

To harness the full potential of real-time analytics in Azure, organizations must have a reliable and scalable means of ingesting streaming data. Azure Event Hubs and Azure IoT Hub serve as the foundational messaging and telemetry ingestion services in the

Azure ecosystem. They are designed to handle massive volumes of data with low latency and high throughput, making them ideal for scenarios like telemetry collection, log streaming, event-driven processing, and IoT integration.

This section explores how Event Hubs and IoT Hub operate, how to configure them, their role in data pipelines, and how they seamlessly integrate with analytics services like Azure Stream Analytics, Azure Data Explorer, Azure Synapse Analytics, and more.

## Azure Event Hubs Overview

Azure Event Hubs is a **big data streaming platform and event ingestion service** capable of receiving and processing millions of events per second. It acts as a data buffer or message broker between event producers and downstream consumers.

**Key Features:**

- High throughput (up to millions of events/sec).
- Partitioned consumer model for scalability.
- Integration with Azure Stream Analytics, Azure Functions, and Kafka-compatible tools.
- Capture to Azure Blob or Data Lake for archival and batch processing.

**Common Producers:**

- Application logs
- Database change feeds

- Web and mobile app telemetry
- System events and diagnostics

---

## Event Hubs Architecture

Event Hubs follows a publish-subscribe pattern:

1. **Producers** send data to an Event Hub.
2. **Partitions** divide the stream for scalability.
3. **Consumer Groups** allow multiple independent readers.
4. **Event Receivers** (like Stream Analytics) pull data from a specific partition and consumer group.

**Conceptual Diagram:**

Producers → Event Hub → Partitions → Consumer Groups → Consumers (ASA, Functions, etc.)

**Partitioning**

- Distributes load across multiple nodes.
- Each partition holds a sequence of messages.
- Producer apps can specify a partition key for ordered events.

---

## Setting Up Event Hubs

### Step 1: Create an Event Hub Namespace

az eventhubs namespace create \

—name mynamespace \

—resource-group myrg \

—location eastus \

—sku Standard

### Step 2: Create an Event Hub

az eventhubs eventhub create \

—name sales-events \

—namespace-name mynamespace \

—resource-group myrg \

—message-retention 7 \

—partition-count 4

### Step 3: Configure Shared Access Policy

az eventhubs eventhub authorization-rule create \

—eventhub-name sales-events \

—namespace-name mynamespace \

—name send-rule \

—resource-group myrg \

—rights Send

## Sending Data to Event Hubs

You can use SDKs in various languages (.NET, Python, Java, Node.js) to publish data.

**Example (Python):**

from azure.eventhub import EventHubProducerClient, EventData

producer = EventHubProducerClient.from_connection_string(conn_str, eventhub_name="sales-events")

event_data_batch = producer.create_batch()

event_data_batch.add(EventData('{"OrderID":123, "Amount":250.00}'))

producer.send_batch(event_data_batch)

## Integrating Event Hubs with Stream Analytics

Once data is flowing into Event Hubs, you can configure it as an input in Azure Stream Analytics to process, filter, and analyze in real time.

**ASA Input Configuration:**

- Source Type: Event Hub
- Connection String: Use SAS policy

- Consumer Group: Specify or create new
- Event Serialization Format: JSON, CSV, Avro

---

## Azure IoT Hub Overview

IoT Hub is a **fully managed bi-directional communication service** between IoT devices and the cloud. It's optimized for secure telemetry collection, command & control, and device management at scale.

**Key Features:**

- Built on Event Hubs for telemetry ingestion.
- Device-to-cloud and cloud-to-device messaging.
- Per-device authentication.
- Device twin for metadata and state management.
- Message routing to custom endpoints (Event Hubs, Blob, etc.).

---

## IoT Hub vs Event Hubs

| Feature | Event Hubs | IoT Hub |
|---|---|---|
| Purpose | General-purpose event ingestion | IoT device communication |
| Built-in device features | None | Yes (device twins, jobs, etc.) |
| Messaging type | One-way (inbound) | Two-way (telemetry + commands) |
| Protocols supported | AMQP, HTTPS, Kafka | AMQP, MQTT, HTTPS |
| Ideal for | Logs, app telemetry | Sensors, industrial equipment |

## Setting Up IoT Hub

### Step 1: Create IoT Hub

```
az iot hub create \
—name myiothub \
—resource-group myrg \
—sku S1 \
—location eastus
```

### Step 2: Register a Device

```
az iot hub device-identity create \
—hub-name myiothub \
```

—device-id device01

**Step 3: Get Connection String**

az iot hub device-identity connection-string show \

—hub-name myiothub \

—device-id device01

## Sending Telemetry from Devices

Use SDKs or command-line tools to simulate device data.

**Example (Python):**

from azure.iot.device import IoTHubDeviceClient, Message

device_client = IoTHubDeviceClient.create_from_connection_string(device_connection_

msg = Message('{"temperature": 23.5, "humidity": 48}')

device_client.send_message(msg)

## Message Routing in IoT Hub

IoT Hub allows you to route messages to downstream services using **message routing rules.**

**Supported Endpoints:**

- Event Hubs
- Azure Storage
- Service Bus

- Azure Functions
- Cosmos DB (via Custom Routing)

Routing conditions can be applied based on message content, properties, or device ID.

---

## Real-Time Processing Pipeline Example

1. IoT devices send telemetry to IoT Hub.
2. IoT Hub routes messages to an Event Hub-compatible endpoint.
3. Azure Stream Analytics ingests from Event Hub.
4. ASA filters high temperature readings.
5. Results are written to:

   ◦ Power BI for dashboards

   ◦ Azure Data Lake for archiving

   ◦ Azure Functions for alerts

---

## Monitoring and Diagnostics

**Event Hubs:**

- Track incoming/outgoing messages per partition.
- Monitor capture activity and delivery errors.

- Integrate with Azure Monitor and Log Analytics.

**IoT Hub:**

- Device connectivity status.
- Message delivery logs.
- Device twin synchronization.
- Alerts on device disconnection or abnormal activity.

---

## Performance and Scaling

**Event Hubs Scaling:**

- Increase **throughput units (TUs)**.
- Scale **partition count** (requires recreation).
- Use **Event Hubs Capture** to auto-archive streams to Blob or ADLS Gen2.

**IoT Hub Scaling:**

- Scale via SKU (S1, S2, S3).
- 400,000 msgs/unit/day (S1).
- Use **message batching** and **compression** on constrained devices.

---

## Security Considerations

- Use **shared access policies** with minimal rights.
- Enable **IP filtering**, **VNet integration**, and **private endpoints**.
- Authenticate IoT devices using **X.509 certificates** or **token-based auth**.
- Encrypt messages end-to-end.

---

## Summary

Azure Event Hubs and IoT Hub are cornerstone services for ingesting real-time data into the Azure analytics ecosystem. Event Hubs offers a high-throughput platform for generic event ingestion, while IoT Hub extends this with device-specific features ideal for managing fleets of connected sensors and devices.

Their integration with services like Azure Stream Analytics, Synapse, and Power BI allows organizations to unlock real-time visibility into operations, automate responses to critical events, and generate value from streaming data at scale.

In the next section, we'll learn how to leverage **Power BI for Real-Time Dashboards**, enabling dynamic visualization of live data streamed from Event Hubs and IoT Hub through Azure Stream Analytics.

# Real-Time Dashboards with Power BI

Real-time dashboards are a powerful way to visualize and interact with streaming data as it flows into your system. Power BI,

Microsoft's flagship business intelligence tool, offers deep integration with Azure services—especially Azure Stream Analytics (ASA)—to enable dynamic, live dashboards that reflect the current state of your data, business, or infrastructure.

This section covers how to design, build, and deploy real-time dashboards using Power BI. We'll explore the architecture, how to integrate ASA with Power BI, streaming dataset types, visuals best suited for live updates, and common troubleshooting and optimization strategies. The goal is to give you the tools and knowledge to build production-grade real-time analytics solutions that combine high-performance backend streaming with responsive, user-friendly frontends.

---

## What is a Real-Time Dashboard?

A real-time dashboard continuously updates its visuals as new data arrives—without requiring manual refreshes. Unlike traditional reports that rely on periodic data loads, real-time dashboards use **streaming datasets** to push data directly to the visuals.

**Use Cases:**

- IoT telemetry monitoring
- Financial tickers and transactions
- Operations control centers
- Social media sentiment trackers
- Live user activity monitoring
- Incident and security response

---

## Power BI Dataset Types

There are three primary dataset types in Power BI that can be used with streaming data:

| Dataset Type | Supports Real-Time | Can Create Reports | Persistent Storage |
|---|---|---|---|
| **Streaming** | Yes | No | No |
| **Push** | Yes | Yes | Yes |
| **Hybrid (Streaming + Push)** | Yes | Yes | Yes |

### Streaming Datasets

- Use only Power BI dashboard tiles (cards, gauges, line charts).
- Do not support historical analysis or custom visuals.
- Most performant for fast updates.

### Push Datasets

- Can be queried, used in reports, and combined with other data.
- Updates less frequently (~1/sec).

### Hybrid Datasets

- Combine benefits of both: real-time updates with report capabilities.

## Architecture of a Real-Time Dashboard

Data Source (IoT Hub / Event Hub / API)

→ Azure Stream Analytics

→ Power BI Streaming Dataset (API)

→ Real-Time Dashboard

ASA handles the transformation and business logic, then pushes summarized or filtered results to Power BI through an authenticated API connection.

---

## Creating a Streaming Dataset in Power BI

1. Go to **Power BI Service (app.powerbi.com)**.
2. Navigate to **My Workspace** > **Datasets**.
3. Click + **Create** > **Streaming Dataset**.
4. Select **API** as the source.
5. Define schema (e.g., DeviceId, Temperature, Timestamp).
6. Enable **historic data analysis** if using push or hybrid datasets.

---

## Configuring Azure Stream Analytics Output to Power BI

Within the Azure Stream Analytics job:

1. Go to the **Outputs** tab.
2. Click + **Add Output** > **Power BI**.
3. Sign in with your Power BI credentials.
4. Select **Workspace**, provide dataset name and table name.
5. Choose **authentication mode**: User Account or Service

Principal.

**Example Output Configuration:**

```
{
"name": "PowerBIOutput",
"type": "PowerBI",
"properties": {
"dataset": "DeviceTelemetry",
"table": "SensorReadings",
"workspace": "OperationsTeam"
}
}
```

## Writing Queries for Power BI Output

Design queries in ASA to push aggregated and filtered data.

**Example: Tumbling Window Aggregation**

```
SELECT
DeviceId,
AVG(Temperature) AS AvgTemp,
MAX(Humidity) AS MaxHumidity,
System.Timestamp AS WindowEnd
FROM
```

IoTInput

GROUP BY

TumblingWindow(second, 10), DeviceId

Push only essential, summarized data to Power BI to reduce load and improve visual responsiveness.

---

## Designing Dashboards in Power BI

Once the streaming dataset is available:

1. Go to **My Workspace > Dashboards**.
2. Click + **Add Tile > Custom Streaming Data**.
3. Select your dataset and configure visuals.

**Visuals that support real-time updates:**

- Line charts (time-series)
- Cards (single value)
- Gauges (threshold-based)
- Clustered bar/column charts
- KPI indicators

**Visual Tips:**

- Limit time range to improve refresh rate.
- Avoid slicers and custom visuals in pure streaming dashboards.

- Use conditional formatting and alerts for attention-grabbing cues.

---

## Combining Real-Time with Historical Context

To analyze trends over time or correlate real-time data with batch analytics:

- Use **Hybrid Datasets** (Streaming + Push).
- Store output in Azure Data Lake or Synapse in parallel.
- Use Power BI **composite models** to merge historical and real-time data sources.

**Example Pattern:**

1. ASA outputs telemetry to Power BI (live).
2. Same ASA job writes raw data to Data Lake.
3. Synapse ETL job aggregates data hourly.
4. Power BI merges real-time and aggregated views.

---

## Alerts and Notifications

Power BI supports **data-driven alerts** for card, gauge, and KPI tiles in dashboards:

1. Click on the tile > **More options (•••)** > **Manage alerts**.
2. Define thresholds and alert conditions.
3. Receive notifications via email or trigger **Power Automate** flows.

**Use Case Example:**

- Temperature > 80°C → Alert sent to field engineer via Teams message.

---

## Troubleshooting and Optimization

**Common Issues:**

| Problem | Solution |
|---|---|
| Data not showing in tile | Check schema match between ASA and Power BI |
| Delayed updates | Reduce data size or frequency |
| Dataset quota exceeded | Switch to hybrid model with archiving |
| ASA job stopped unexpectedly | Review logs and monitor outputs |
| Power BI auth expired | Reauthorize output in ASA job settings |

**Performance Tips:**

- Stream only relevant fields.
- Use tumbling windows instead of hopping where possible.
- Keep dashboard visuals simple and lightweight.
- Enable error policies in ASA to drop or log malformed records.

---

## Real-World Examples

### Case 1: Smart Factory Dashboard

- IoT sensors send vibration and temperature data.
- ASA filters for anomalies and aggregates by machine.
- Power BI shows uptime, error rate, and alerts in real time.

### Case 2: Retail Sales Tracking

- POS systems push sales events to Event Hub.
- ASA calculates total revenue and customer wait time.
- Power BI shows per-store KPIs and comparisons.

### Case 3: Security Event Monitoring

- Firewall logs streamed to Event Hub.
- ASA detects failed login spikes and unauthorized access attempts.
- Power BI displays alerts, trends, and maps of threat origins.

---

## Summary

Real-time dashboards in Power BI empower businesses to react faster, improve operational visibility, and drive smarter decisions. By integrating Power BI with Azure Stream Analytics, Event Hubs, and IoT Hub, you can deliver rich, responsive visualizations built directly on top of live data streams.

Whether you're monitoring factory performance, customer behavior, or cloud infrastructure, real-time dashboards provide an essential interface between raw data and actionable insights. The next section will explore additional **use cases and performance tips**, showcasing how real-time analytics solutions can be fine-tuned and deployed at enterprise scale.

## Use Cases and Performance Tips

Real-time analytics is not just a trend—it's a fundamental requirement for businesses that operate in dynamic, data-driven environments. From monitoring logistics fleets and manufacturing lines to detecting fraud and analyzing social media sentiment, real-time data processing opens the door to agility and operational intelligence.

In this section, we will explore real-world use cases of real-time analytics in Azure, demonstrating how services like Azure Stream Analytics, Event Hubs, IoT Hub, and Power BI are used in concert to solve critical business problems. We'll also review essential performance tuning strategies, architectural patterns, and operational best practices to ensure your real-time pipelines are both reliable and scalable.

## Real-Time Analytics Use Cases

### 1. Predictive Maintenance in Manufacturing

**Scenario:** Industrial equipment sensors send telemetry including temperature, vibration, pressure, and operational hours. The manufacturer wants to anticipate equipment failures before they occur.

**Solution Architecture:**

- IoT Hub ingests telemetry from connected machinery.
- Azure Stream Analytics processes data using sliding windows to detect anomalies.
- Azure Machine Learning model is called via UDF to predict failure probability.
- High-risk events trigger alerts through Azure Functions.
- Power BI displays equipment status and risk levels.

**ASA Query Example:**

```
SELECT
DeviceId,
AVG(Vibration) AS AvgVibration,
System.Timestamp AS WindowEnd
FROM
```

SensorStream

GROUP BY

SlidingWindow(minute, 10, 1), DeviceId

**Benefits:**

- Reduced downtime
- Increased asset lifespan
- Improved worker safety

---

**2. Real-Time Fraud Detection**

**Scenario:** A financial services company wants to monitor transactions for suspicious patterns, such as excessive withdrawals, location anomalies, or known fraud signatures.

**Solution Architecture:**

- Event Hubs receives real-time transaction streams.
- ASA performs rule-based filtering and pattern recognition.
- Azure ML or Synapse scoring predicts fraud probability.
- Suspect transactions are pushed to Service Bus for downstream workflows.
- Dashboard shows live fraud alerts by geography and risk level.

**Key Features Used:**

- Geospatial functions (STDistance, STWithin)
- Session windows
- Power BI real-time tiles

**Alert Trigger Example:**

```
SELECT
CustomerId,
COUNT(*) AS AttemptCount,
System.Timestamp AS WindowEnd
FROM
Transactions
WHERE
Location <> LastKnownLocation
GROUP BY
SessionWindow(minute, 15), CustomerId
HAVING COUNT(*) > 3
```

---

**3. Supply Chain and Logistics Monitoring**

**Scenario:** A logistics provider tracks hundreds of delivery vehicles and wants to monitor delivery times, optimize routes, and prevent SLA breaches.

**Solution Architecture:**

- GPS and status data are sent to IoT Hub.
- ASA analyzes delays, traffic trends, and vehicle idle times.
- Power BI presents delivery statuses, ETAs, and route metrics.
- Alerts trigger if a package is delayed beyond threshold.

**Enhancements:**

- Integrate with Azure Maps for route visualization.
- Include weather data for predictive rerouting.

---

### 4. Live Customer Interaction Analytics

**Scenario:** An e-commerce company wants to monitor user behavior on their website to personalize experiences and identify product interest in real-time.

**Solution Architecture:**

- Web events pushed to Event Hubs via JavaScript SDK.
- ASA aggregates session activity per user.
- Real-time scoring for recommending content.
- Heatmaps and funnel analysis in Power BI.

**Use Case Benefits:**

- Increased conversion rates
- Reduced bounce rate
- Real-time marketing intervention

---

**5. Social Media Sentiment Tracking**

**Scenario:** A marketing team wants to monitor live brand mentions and sentiment across Twitter.

**Solution Architecture:**

- Tweets ingested via Logic Apps or custom API.
- ASA extracts hashtags, user mentions, and sentiment (via Azure Cognitive Services).
- Power BI presents live feeds and sentiment trends.
- Keywords triggering negative sentiment alerts routed to support teams.

**Challenges:**

- Handling unstructured, varied data
- Rate-limited APIs
- Language detection and context disambiguation

---

## Performance Tips for Real-Time Pipelines

### 1. Partitioning Strategy

Use Event Hub partitioning aligned with consumer parallelism in ASA or Functions to:

- Maximize throughput
- Avoid data skew
- Enable event ordering per key (e.g., CustomerId)

**ASA Guidance:**

- Use partition key wisely to evenly distribute load.
- Set SU allocation based on partition count.

### 2. Query Optimization in Azure Stream Analytics

- **Filter early**: Apply WHERE clauses before joins or aggregations.
- **Avoid unnecessary joins**: Push lookup logic to reference data if possible.
- **Use appropriate windows**: Choose tumbling for strict windows, hopping for overlaps, and session for variable-length grouping.

### 3. Minimize Output Volume

- Output only necessary fields to Power BI or databases.

- Compress and batch writes where supported (e.g., Parquet to ADLS).
- Limit data frequency for visuals to avoid overload (e.g., every 5–10 seconds).

**4. Stream Analytics Unit (SU) Tuning**

- Start small, then scale up based on:
  - Input events/sec
  - Query complexity
  - Output latency requirements

**Example CLI Update:**

az stream-analytics job update \

—name OrderInsightsJob \

—resource-group analytics-rg \

—streaming-units 6

**5. Avoid Event Duplication**

- Ensure each event has a unique identifier (e.g., GUID or composite key).
- Deduplicate using ASA or downstream database logic.

---

## Operational Best Practices

### Monitoring

- Enable diagnostic logging for ASA and Event Hubs.
- Create custom metrics in Azure Monitor (e.g., event lag, dropped messages).
- Use Log Analytics for historical query performance review.

### Alerting

- Trigger alerts on:
  - Backlog growth
  - Output failures
  - SU capacity breach
  - Query exceptions

### Resilience

- Use retry and fallback logic in outputs (e.g., to SQL or storage).
- Store raw telemetry in ADLS for replay or recovery.
- Monitor SHIR (if used) for availability in hybrid integrations.

**CI/CD and Automation**

- Use ARM templates or Bicep to define ASA jobs.
- Store query logic and configurations in version control.
- Integrate deployments with Azure DevOps or GitHub Actions.

---

## Summary

Real-time data analytics opens the door to operational agility, customer responsiveness, and predictive capabilities across industries. Whether it's detecting fraud before it occurs, rerouting a delivery in response to a traffic jam, or alerting a support team to a surge in negative sentiment, the value of reacting in the moment cannot be overstated.

Azure provides a mature, scalable toolkit to support such initiatives. By combining Event Hubs, IoT Hub, Azure Stream Analytics, Power BI, and Synapse, you can create powerful real-time architectures tailored to your use case.

Optimizing performance, tuning query logic, and operationalizing monitoring are essential steps in taking your real-time pipelines from proof-of-concept to production. In the next chapter, we'll zoom out and explore how to bring together everything we've covered so far to **design unified, end-to-end analytics solutions** using the Azure data platform.

# Chapter 7: Building End-to-End Analytics Solutions

## Designing a Unified Data Strategy

Designing a unified data strategy is critical for organizations aiming to maximize the value of their data assets across the enterprise. An effective strategy goes beyond tool selection—it aligns people, processes, and technology to ensure data is collected, governed, integrated, and analyzed efficiently and securely. In Azure, this means bringing together a suite of services like Azure Data Factory, Azure Data Lake Storage, Synapse Analytics, Azure SQL, Azure Stream Analytics, and Power BI into a cohesive platform that supports both batch and real-time workloads.

This section explores the fundamental principles of a unified data strategy, architectural patterns for implementation on Azure, organizational alignment considerations, governance and security, and best practices for ensuring scalability and performance. We'll also examine how modern analytics requirements—like self-service BI, data democratization, and machine learning—fit into the strategic blueprint.

---

### Key Elements of a Unified Data Strategy

A well-rounded data strategy incorporates several core components:

1. **Data Ingestion** – Bringing data from disparate sources into a centralized location.
2. **Data Storage** – Organizing data in a secure, scalable, and accessible manner.
3. **Data Processing** – Applying transformations, enrichment,

and modeling to raw data.

4. **Data Access and Visualization** – Enabling stakeholders to explore and act on data.
5. **Governance and Security** – Ensuring data integrity, compliance, and access control.
6. **Advanced Analytics** – Supporting AI/ML workloads with integrated infrastructure.

Each layer in this model builds upon the previous one, forming an integrated pipeline from source to insight.

---

## Designing for Azure: Logical Architecture

Let's explore a typical Azure-centric data architecture that supports both operational and analytical workloads:

1. **Sources:**

○ On-prem SQL/Oracle databases

○ Cloud services (Salesforce, SAP, Dynamics)

○ IoT devices (via IoT Hub)

○ Streaming sources (Event Hubs)

2. **Ingestion Layer:**

○ **Azure Data Factory** for batch data.

○ **Azure Stream Analytics** for real-time data.

3. **Storage Layer:**

○ **Azure Data Lake Storage Gen2** (raw, curated, and trusted zones).

○ **Azure Blob Storage** for archival.

○ **SQL Pools** in Synapse for structured data marts.

4. **Processing Layer:**

○ **Data Flows** in ADF for transformations.

○ **Synapse SQL / Spark** for big data and model scoring.

○ **Azure Functions / Logic Apps** for orchestration.

5. **Semantic and Visualization Layer:**

○ **Power BI** for dashboards and self-service reporting.

○ **Synapse Studio** for integrated development.

○ **Azure Purview** for cataloging and data lineage.

6. **Advanced Analytics Layer:**

○ **Azure Machine Learning** for model training and deployment.

○ **Synapse ML / Spark** for in-pipeline scoring.

---

## Storage Zone Strategy

A unified strategy segments the lake into logical zones:

1. **Raw Zone:** Direct dumps from source systems in native

format.

2. **Curated Zone:** Cleaned, structured, and enriched data with standardized schema.
3. **Trusted Zone:** Final datasets used for reporting and ML—optimized for performance.

**Benefits:**

- Decouples raw ingestion from consumption.
- Enables time-travel and rollback.
- Supports compliance via data retention policies.

---

## Data Modeling and Warehousing

A unified strategy includes structured data models for business consumption:

- **Star and Snowflake schemas** in Synapse SQL pools.
- **Fact and dimension tables** based on subject areas.
- **Materialized views** for frequently accessed aggregates.
- **CDC and incremental loading** strategies.

**ELT Example in Synapse:**

```
INSERT INTO fact_sales (order_id, customer_id, total_amount)

SELECT order_id, customer_id, amount

FROM staging_sales
```

```
WHERE load_date = CAST(GETDATE() AS DATE)
```

---

## Orchestration and Scheduling

Automating workflows is crucial for reliability.

- **Data Factory Pipelines** coordinate batch loads and transformations.
- **Triggers** schedule or event-enable jobs (e.g., when a file arrives).
- **Synapse Pipelines** integrate data movement, Spark, SQL, and ML.

**Common Patterns:**

- Daily ingestion and processing jobs.
- Near-real-time telemetry pipelines.
- Event-driven response to fraud or SLA breaches.

---

## Enabling Self-Service and Democratized Analytics

Empowering end-users to analyze data securely:

- **Power BI workspaces** for departmental reporting.
- **Azure Active Directory** for role-based access.
- **Shared semantic models** with reusable measures.
- **Governed data marts** published in Synapse or Power BI.

**Best Practice:** Use **row-level security (RLS)** and **object-level security (OLS)** in Synapse and Power BI to protect sensitive data.

---

## Governance and Compliance

Data strategy must align with legal, ethical, and regulatory standards:

- **Azure Purview** for data cataloging, lineage, and classification.
- **Audit Logs** in Synapse and ADF for traceability.
- **Data Loss Prevention (DLP)** rules in Power BI.
- **Encryption at rest and in transit** with customer-managed keys.
- **Policy enforcement** via Azure Policy and Blueprints.

---

## Scalability and Performance Considerations

1. **Partitioning**: Divide large tables/files for parallel access.
2. **Caching**: Use Synapse result set caching and Spark in-memory caching.
3. **Query Optimization**: Leverage statistics, indexes, and columnstore formats.
4. **Cost Optimization**: Use serverless pools for ad-hoc queries and scale-down idle resources.

---

## Building for Change and Innovation

Future-proofing your strategy requires agility:

- Modular architecture enables plug-and-play service swaps.
- Use **parameterized pipelines** and **templated notebooks** for reusability.
- Embrace **data contracts** and **schema versioning** to reduce downstream impact.
- Maintain **CI/CD pipelines** for data platform artifacts.

---

## Organizational Alignment

People and process are as important as tools:

- Establish **data product owners** per domain.
- Use **DataOps** principles for automation and monitoring.
- Train end-users in Power BI, SQL, and Synapse usage.
- Create **Center of Excellence (CoE)** teams for governance and evangelism.

---

## Example: Retail Company Data Strategy

**Scenario:** A retail company operates 200 stores and wants to unify POS, inventory, and customer engagement data.

**Implementation:**

- Daily POS batch loads via ADF.

- Live inventory updates via Event Hub and ASA.
- Synapse SQL stores curated views for regional and product-level reporting.
- Azure ML forecasts demand using historical data from the trusted zone.
- Executives use Power BI dashboards across HQ and mobile devices.

**Benefits:**

- Unified 360-degree view of customers and operations.
- Optimized inventory levels.
- Reduced reporting delays from 24 hours to real time.

---

## Summary

A unified data strategy in Azure is not a single service or product—it's a mindset and framework for delivering trusted, timely, and actionable insights at scale. It orchestrates data ingestion, storage, processing, access, and governance in a coherent architecture that meets the needs of both IT and business stakeholders.

With a flexible yet disciplined approach, organizations can future-proof their data investments, improve decision-making, and enable innovation across the enterprise. In the following sections, we'll see how these concepts come together in real-world scenarios—starting with the combination of Synapse, SQL, and Data Factory in integrated analytics pipelines.

# Combining SQL, Synapse, and Data Factory

Modern data platforms require flexibility, performance, and the ability to scale across massive data volumes. In Azure, this need is met by combining three core services—**Azure SQL**, **Azure Synapse Analytics**, and **Azure Data Factory**—to build robust, scalable, and integrated analytics solutions. Each service has its strengths, and when orchestrated together, they form a comprehensive foundation for modern data warehousing, ETL/ELT processes, real-time analytics, and business intelligence.

This section explores how to integrate and operationalize these services effectively, covering data ingestion, transformation, warehousing, reporting, and orchestration patterns. We'll also address key design principles, code examples, deployment models, and operational best practices to enable enterprise-grade analytics solutions.

---

## Role of Each Service in the Analytics Stack

| Service | Role |
|---|---|
| Azure Data Factory | Data ingestion, movement, transformation, orchestration |
| Azure Synapse Analytics | Scalable MPP data warehouse + big data analytics |
| Azure SQL Database | Transactional store, lightweight analytics, source system |

By combining the strengths of each, you can:

- Use **SQL Database** for OLTP and operational reporting.

- Use **Data Factory** to orchestrate and transform data at scale.

- Use **Synapse** for complex queries, aggregations, and serving models to BI tools.

---

## Ingesting Data Using Data Factory

**Azure Data Factory (ADF)** is the central orchestration layer. It connects to hundreds of sources—including on-prem, cloud, structured, semi-structured, and unstructured systems.

**Example: Ingest Data from Azure SQL to Data Lake**

1. **Linked Service** – Define source (Azure SQL) and sink (ADLS Gen2).
2. **Dataset** – Point to the source table and sink path.
3. **Copy Activity** – Transfers the data in a pipeline.

```
{
"name": "CopySqlToLake",
"type": "Copy",
"inputs": [{"referenceName": "SalesSQLDataset"}],
"outputs": [{"referenceName": "SalesADLSDataset"}],
"typeProperties": {
"source": { "type": "SqlSource" },
"sink": { "type": "ParquetSink" }
```

}

}

This pattern is used to land data in the **raw** zone of your lake.

## Transforming Data with Mapping Data Flows or SQL Scripts

After ingestion, transformations are applied either in ADF Mapping Data Flows or within Synapse SQL pools.

**Option 1: Use Mapping Data Flows in ADF**

Visual design, Spark-powered, ideal for:

- Cleansing and enrichment
- Joining multiple sources
- Filtering, aggregating, and reshaping

**Option 2: Use SQL Scripts in Synapse**

For structured data, T-SQL inside Synapse SQL pools provides performance and flexibility.

—Aggregate daily sales

CREATE OR ALTER VIEW vw_DailySales AS

SELECT

CAST(OrderDate AS DATE) AS SaleDate,

SUM(TotalAmount) AS TotalSales,

COUNT(*) AS OrderCount

FROM SalesCurated

GROUP BY CAST(OrderDate AS DATE)

Run this transformation via **Stored Procedure Activity** or **SQL Script Activity** in ADF or Synapse Pipelines.

---

## Loading into Synapse Dedicated SQL Pool

Once data is cleaned, it is loaded into a **star schema** inside Synapse SQL dedicated pool for reporting.

**Dimensional Model Example:**

- fact_sales (fact)
- dim_customer, dim_product, dim_store (dimensions)

**Create Table Example:**

CREATE TABLE fact_sales

(

SaleID BIGINT,

CustomerID INT,

ProductID INT,

StoreID INT,

SaleDate DATE,

Quantity INT,

```
TotalAmount DECIMAL(18,2)
)
WITH
(
DISTRIBUTION = HASH(SaleID),
CLUSTERED COLUMNSTORE INDEX
);
```

## Orchestrating the Workflow

Use **Data Factory Pipelines** or **Synapse Pipelines** to orchestrate end-to-end flow.

**Example Pipeline: Daily Sales ETL**

1. Copy Activity: Azure SQL → ADLS Gen2 (raw zone)
2. Data Flow Activity: Clean and enrich → curated zone
3. Stored Procedure Activity: Load to fact_sales
4. Execute Power BI dataset refresh via REST API

Add **parameters** and **triggers** to make this reusable across regions, product lines, or environments.

## Using Serverless SQL for Exploratory Analysis

**Synapse Serverless SQL Pools** allow querying files directly in the lake without loading into a warehouse.

```
SELECT
ProductID,
```

SUM(Amount) AS TotalAmount

FROM

OPENROWSET(

BULK 'https://mydatalake.dfs.core.windows.net/curated/sales/*.parquet',

FORMAT='PARQUET'

) AS sales

GROUP BY ProductID

Great for:

- Ad hoc analytics
- Power BI quick dashboards
- Data validation in pipelines

---

## Power BI and Semantic Models

The final output of most analytics pipelines is business-facing dashboards.

- Create **views or materialized views** in Synapse SQL for Power BI to consume.
- Use **DirectQuery** for up-to-date data or **import mode** for performance.
- Secure using **row-level security (RLS)** tied to AAD groups.

**Power BI Dataset Refresh Automation:**

Use REST API within ADF or Synapse Pipeline Web Activity:

```
{
"method": "POST",
"url": "https://api.powerbi.com/v1.0/myorg/groups/{group_id}/datasets/{dataset_id}/refreshes",
"headers": {
"Content-Type": "application/json",
"Authorization": "Bearer {token}"
}
}
```

## Monitoring and Logging

**Data Factory / Synapse Pipelines:**

- Built-in monitoring dashboards
- Retry and timeout settings
- Integration with Azure Monitor and Log Analytics

**SQL Monitoring:**

- Query performance insights in Synapse Studio
- Dynamic Management Views (DMVs) for workload tracking

- Resource usage metrics (DWUs, tempdb, memory grants)

**Example DMV Query:**

```
SELECT
request_id,
total_elapsed_time,
command,
status
FROM sys.dm_pdw_exec_requests
ORDER BY total_elapsed_time DESC
```

---

## Best Practices

1. **Separate raw, curated, and trusted zones** using ADLS folder structure.
2. **Parameterize everything**: File paths, table names, dates.
3. **Use schema drift** in Mapping Data Flows for evolving sources.
4. **Partition large Synapse tables** by date or geography.
5. **Use stored procedures for complex transformations**, not row-by-row logic.
6. **Use Synapse SQL views as semantic layer** for Power BI.
7. **Enable caching** for serverless queries and monitor cost impact.

---

## Real-World Scenario: eCommerce Sales Analytics

**Goal:** Deliver daily and real-time insights into orders, customer behavior, and revenue performance.

**Pipeline:**

1. Azure SQL holds order transactions.
2. ADF copies and stores raw data in ADLS Gen2.
3. Mapping Data Flows enrich with customer and product info.
4. Data is loaded into Synapse fact_sales and dim_customer.
5. Power BI reads from Synapse views for executive dashboard.
6. ADF triggers refresh nightly, with ASA feeding live updates hourly.

**Outcome:**

- Unified batch + real-time insights.
- Scalable to millions of transactions.
- Role-based access and audit compliance.

---

## Summary

By combining Azure SQL, Synapse Analytics, and Data Factory, organizations can create robust, scalable, and maintainable data solutions. Data Factory serves as the integration and orchestration layer, Synapse as the scalable analytical engine, and SQL databases as either sources or lightweight reporting stores. Together, they support the full analytics lifecycle—from raw ingestion to curated business insights.

In the next section, we'll explore how to apply these tools in a real-world context with a detailed case study of a retail analytics platform, demonstrating implementation patterns and architectural decisions across the stack.

## Case Study: Retail Analytics Platform

Retail is one of the most data-rich industries, characterized by high-frequency transactions, complex supply chains, and rapidly changing consumer behavior. Leveraging data effectively in this environment is crucial for competitive advantage. In this case study, we examine the design, implementation, and optimization of a comprehensive retail analytics platform using Azure's data services. We will explore how Azure Data Factory, Azure Synapse Analytics, Power BI, and other supporting services work together to deliver real-time and historical insights for a fictional retail company—**Contoso Retail**.

---

### Business Requirements

Contoso Retail operates a chain of physical stores and an e-commerce platform. The company's goals are:

- Unify data from in-store POS systems and online sales portals.
- Track sales performance and customer behavior across channels.
- Forecast product demand and optimize inventory.
- Enable real-time monitoring of transactions.

- Provide executives and managers with interactive dashboards.
- Ensure data security and compliance with GDPR and PCI-DSS.

---

## Architecture Overview

Contoso's data architecture follows a **hub-and-spoke** model, with Azure Synapse Analytics as the central data platform, orchestrated by Azure Data Factory and visualized through Power BI.

**Core Components:**

1. **Azure Data Factory (ADF)** – ETL/ELT orchestration
2. **Azure Data Lake Storage Gen2 (ADLS Gen2)** – Data lake for raw, curated, and trusted zones
3. **Azure Synapse Analytics** – Analytical engine and semantic model
4. **Azure SQL Database** – POS system backend
5. **Event Hubs** – Ingestion of real-time web transactions
6. **Azure Stream Analytics (ASA)** – Processing live order data
7. **Power BI** – Dashboards and reporting

---

## Data Sources and Ingestion

**Batch Sources:**

- **In-store POS systems**: Daily exports pushed to a secure FTP and ingested by ADF.

- **Online orders database**: Azure SQL Database containing real-time order events.

- **Customer CRM**: Salesforce API with customer demographics and loyalty data.

**Streaming Sources:**

- **E-commerce interactions**: Browsing and cart events via Event Hubs.

- **Payment processing gateway**: Real-time payment confirmation.

**Ingestion Pattern:**

1. ADF copies daily POS CSVs from FTP to ADLS Gen2 /raw/pos/.
2. ADF extracts new orders from SQL Database and writes them to /raw/online_orders/.
3. ASA ingests data from Event Hubs and writes summarized data into /curated/real_time_orders/.

---

## Transformation and Enrichment

**Curated Layer Pipeline (ADF Mapping Data Flow):**

1. **POS Data Transformation**

○ Schema standardization

○ Currency normalization

  - Join with product dimension for enrichment

2. **Customer Data Enrichment**
  - Join with loyalty and segmentation attributes
  - Mask PII fields using derived columns

```
iif(isNull(CustomerEmail), 'unknown', hash(CustomerEmail))
```

3. **Sales Aggregation**
  - Aggregate sales by store, product category, and time
  - Append to curated Parquet dataset in ADLS

**Trusted Layer Processing:**

1. ADF triggers Synapse Stored Procedure to load data from /curated/ into fact_sales, dim_store, dim_product, dim_customer.

```
INSERT INTO fact_sales
SELECT
OrderID, CustomerID, ProductID, StoreID, Quantity, TotalAmount, OrderDate
FROM curated.sales_flatfile
WHERE LoadDate = CAST(GETDATE() AS DATE)
```

1. Incremental load using watermark column for new records only.

## Real-Time Analytics with Azure Stream Analytics

ASA job processes online transactions with a 10-second tumbling window to monitor conversion rates and alert for high-value transactions.

```
SELECT

UserId,

COUNT(*) AS Transactions,

SUM(OrderValue) AS TotalSpent

FROM

EcomStream

GROUP BY

TumblingWindow(second, 10), UserId
```

- Output 1: Writes live data to Power BI for executive dashboard.
- Output 2: Writes to ADLS Gen2 /curated/realtime_dashboard/ for archival and backfill.

---

## Data Warehousing in Synapse

Contoso's Synapse SQL pool hosts a star schema for BI consumption.

- **Fact Tables**: fact_sales, fact_inventory, fact_web_activity

- **Dimension Tables:** dim_product, dim_store, dim_customer, dim_time

Tables use **Hash-distribution** on OrderID or CustomerID for performance.

**Table Design Example:**

```
CREATE TABLE dim_customer (
CustomerID INT PRIMARY KEY,
FirstName NVARCHAR(50),
LastName NVARCHAR(50),
Region NVARCHAR(50),
LoyaltyTier NVARCHAR(20),
EmailHash NVARCHAR(256)
)
WITH (
DISTRIBUTION = ROUND_ROBIN,
CLUSTERED COLUMNSTORE INDEX
)
```

## Business Intelligence with Power BI

Power BI workspaces are created per department (Sales, Operations, Finance). Shared datasets are built from Synapse views.

**Sales Dashboard Features:**

- Daily revenue by region
- Top-selling products
- Inventory levels vs demand forecast
- Real-time order ticker from ASA

**Row-Level Security Example:**

—RLS rule for Store Managers

[UserStoreID] = LOOKUPVALUE(dim_store.StoreID, dim_store.ManagerEmail, USERNAME())

- Synced with Azure AD
- Audit logs tracked via Power BI Activity Log

---

## Monitoring and Automation

**Data Factory:**

- Triggers nightly batch ETL.
- Retry logic for FTP or API connection issues.
- Alert on pipeline failure via Azure Monitor.

**Synapse:**

- Query performance insights monitored daily.
- Dedicated pool scaled up/down based on schedule.

- Caching enabled for frequently queried views.

ASA:

- Stream lag and output errors tracked.
- Backpressure alerts configured.
- Data archived to lake for reprocessing if needed.

---

## Security and Compliance

- **Azure Key Vault** manages credentials for ADF and ASA.
- **Private Endpoints** used for SQL and Synapse to isolate network access.
- **Encryption** in transit and at rest with CMKs.
- **Purview** catalogs all datasets with sensitivity labels.

---

## Cost Optimization Measures

- Serverless SQL used for ad-hoc and preview queries.
- Synapse compute auto-paused during non-business hours.
- Power BI Premium workspaces used for scalable refresh schedules.
- Data Lifecycle Management applied to ADLS zones:

- ○ Raw zone retention: 30 days
- ○ Curated zone: 90 days
- ○ Trusted zone: Indefinite

---

## Outcomes

Contoso Retail achieved the following results:

- Unified data from 3 systems in under 2 weeks.
- Reduced dashboard refresh time from 12 hours to 5 minutes.
- Forecasting accuracy improved by 22% using integrated ML.
- Enabled 40+ business users with secure, self-service analytics.

---

## Summary

This case study illustrates how a retail enterprise can modernize its analytics stack by leveraging Azure's integrated platform. With Data Factory orchestrating movement, Synapse acting as the analytical engine, ASA enabling real-time insights, and Power BI delivering rich dashboards, the architecture meets both operational and strategic needs.

As seen here, best practices around security, governance, modular architecture, and cost control are essential for success. The next section explores a similar case in the healthcare domain, where data sensitivity and compliance require additional design considerations.

## Case Study: Healthcare Data Lake Implementation

Healthcare organizations are among the most data-intensive and highly regulated institutions. From patient records and lab results to medical imaging and wearable telemetry, the volume and complexity of data is vast. In this case study, we examine how a healthcare provider—**NorthHealth Clinics**—implemented a secure, scalable, and compliant data lake architecture in Azure. This platform not only unified fragmented clinical and operational data sources but also enabled advanced analytics, machine learning, and regulatory reporting.

---

### Objectives and Challenges

NorthHealth Clinics aimed to modernize their analytics infrastructure with the following goals:

- Centralize data from EHR (Electronic Health Record), imaging systems, and patient engagement tools.
- Ensure HIPAA compliance and support other regulatory requirements.
- Enable clinicians and data scientists to explore and analyze data securely.
- Support predictive models for patient readmission and treatment optimization.

- Allow integration with third-party applications and data vendors.

**Challenges:**

- Legacy systems with no modern APIs.
- Strict data privacy regulations (HIPAA, GDPR).
- Large volumes of semi-structured and unstructured data (e.g., clinical notes, PDFs, HL7 messages).
- Diverse user personas: clinicians, data scientists, compliance teams.

---

## Architecture Overview

The architecture at NorthHealth is based on the Azure Data Lake paradigm, utilizing structured zones for ingestion, curation, and analytics. Security, data classification, and governance are deeply integrated.

**Core Components:**

1. **Azure Data Factory (ADF)** – Ingest data from EMRs, SFTP, and APIs.
2. **Azure Data Lake Storage Gen2** – Store data across raw, curated, and trusted zones.
3. **Azure Synapse Analytics** – Perform structured analysis, build data marts.
4. **Azure Databricks** – Prepare data for ML and run advanced analytics.
5. **Azure Purview** – Govern data cataloging and lineage.

6. **Azure Key Vault** – Manage secrets and connection strings.
7. **Azure Private Link** – Secure communication between services.
8. **Azure Monitor & Log Analytics** – Centralized auditing and diagnostics.

---

## Data Ingestion Strategy

NorthHealth receives data from multiple systems:

- **EHR System (Epic)**: HL7 messages sent to an integration server.
- **Laboratory Systems**: CSV files pushed daily to SFTP.
- **Imaging Systems (PACS)**: DICOM files ingested via blob API.
- **Wearables & Patient Apps**: RESTful APIs exposing patient-generated health data.

ADF was used with a combination of:

- **SFTP connectors** for lab data.
- **REST connectors** for mobile app APIs.
- **Event-based triggers** for real-time HL7 feed ingestion.
- **Custom .NET Azure Functions** for handling legacy flat files and HL7 parsing.

All ingested data lands in the **raw zone** of the Data Lake in its original format.

## Data Zone Structure and Organization

The data lake is logically segmented into three main zones:

**1. Raw Zone:**

- Immutable data as received from source.
- Organized by source system and date.
- Format: CSV, JSON, XML, HL7, PDF, DICOM

**2. Curated Zone:**

- Standardized schemas.
- PHI masked or tokenized.
- Structural consistency enforced.
- Stored in Parquet for efficient querying.

**3. Trusted Zone:**

- Ready-to-use datasets for analytics, BI, and ML.
- Integrated across sources.
- Validated for completeness and integrity.

**Naming Convention Example:**

/curated/lab_results/2025/04/25/lab_results.parquet

## Transformation and Standardization

Transformations are performed using a mix of **ADF Mapping Data Flows** and **Azure Databricks Notebooks**, depending on the data type and complexity.

**PHI Masking:**

```
iif(isNull(PatientSSN), null, sha2(PatientSSN, 256))
```

**Clinical Code Mapping:**

- ICD-10 to SNOMED mapping table stored in Synapse.
- Applied during transformation in Databricks for free-text data.

**Unstructured Data Handling:**

- Clinical notes ingested as PDFs and parsed using Azure Form Recognizer.
- NLP applied using Databricks and Azure Cognitive Services for:
  - Entity recognition (e.g., medications, symptoms)
  - Sentiment analysis (e.g., patient mood)

---

## Synapse Analytics for Structured Reporting

Synapse SQL pools host data marts tailored to various departments:

- **Clinical Operations**: Appointments, patient wait times, staffing KPIs.
- **Population Health**: Readmission rates, chronic illness trends, social determinants.
- **Compliance**: Data access logs, audit events, sharing activities.

**Example: Hospital Stay Metrics**

```
SELECT
HospitalID,
COUNT(*) AS Admissions,
AVG(DATEDIFF(day, AdmissionDate, DischargeDate)) AS AvgLOS
FROM
fact_admissions
WHERE
DischargeDate >= DATEADD(day, -30, GETDATE())
GROUP BY
HospitalID
```

Synapse views are published as semantic models to Power BI.

## Machine Learning Integration

Azure Databricks notebooks use curated zone data to:

- Train models for patient readmission prediction.
- Segment patients for chronic care management.
- Evaluate model fairness across demographics.

**Workflow:**

1. Extract and clean data from Data Lake.
2. Train logistic regression and XGBoost models.
3. Register models in Azure ML.
4. Batch score new admissions daily.
5. Output predictions into trusted/risk_scores/ for consumption by clinicians.

---

## Governance and Compliance

**Azure Purview:**

- All datasets classified automatically (e.g., PHI, PII, diagnosis codes).
- Sensitivity labels applied.
- Data lineage from source to Power BI visible.

**Access Control:**

- Role-based access enforced via Azure AD and Synapse security.
- Token-based access to APIs.

- Private endpoints and IP restrictions limit external exposure.

**Auditing:**

- Log Analytics centralizes pipeline execution, SQL activity, and data access logs.
- Alerts configured for data exfiltration risks or anomalous access patterns.

---

## Visualization and Reporting

Power BI dashboards are provided for:

- **Executives**: KPI snapshots, operational metrics.
- **Clinicians**: Patient histories, treatment timelines.
- **Public Health**: Aggregated trends across regions.

**Power BI Features Used:**

- Row-level security (RLS) per physician or department.
- Composite models combining live Synapse and import-mode datasets.
- Embedded reports in custom clinician portal via Power BI REST API.

---

## Deployment and Automation

- **ARM Templates** and **Bicep** for infrastructure-as-code.
- **DevOps Pipelines** automate deployment of pipelines, notebooks, and SQL scripts.
- **QA/Dev/Prod Environments** with separate resource groups and data partitions.

---

## Results and Impact

NorthHealth Clinics reported:

- 50% faster generation of compliance reports.
- 95% accuracy in automated PHI de-identification.
- Real-time visibility into bed utilization and resource allocation.
- Significant reduction in manual data prep for data science teams.

The platform also enabled them to partner with universities and researchers via secure, anonymized datasets.

---

## Summary

The NorthHealth case study demonstrates how a healthcare provider can modernize and unify its data landscape using Azure Data Lake architecture. The key success factors included clear data zoning, strong governance, advanced analytics, and automation across the lifecycle.

By combining services like ADF, Synapse, Databricks, and Power BI, and aligning them with regulatory requirements, NorthHealth successfully delivered a compliant, scalable, and future-proof data analytics solution. In doing so, they improved patient care, operational efficiency, and enabled new data-driven innovation.

# Chapter 8: Advanced Analytics and Machine Learning in Azure

## Integrating Azure ML with Synapse

Machine learning (ML) is rapidly becoming a cornerstone of modern analytics strategies. It enables organizations to go beyond descriptive and diagnostic analytics into predictive and prescriptive capabilities. In the Azure ecosystem, **Azure Machine Learning (Azure ML)** and **Azure Synapse Analytics** provide a powerful combination for integrating ML into your data platform. This section explores how to bring these services together to build and operationalize machine learning models at scale using a unified architecture.

We will explore integration patterns, development workflows, deployment strategies, governance considerations, and use cases, ensuring your organization can embed ML insights seamlessly into existing data pipelines, BI dashboards, and applications.

---

### Key Components of Integration

1. **Azure Machine Learning (Azure ML)**
   A cloud-based service for developing, training, managing, and deploying ML models. It supports frameworks like Scikit-learn, PyTorch, TensorFlow, and integrates tightly with other Azure services.
2. **Azure Synapse Analytics**
   A unified platform for data integration, warehousing, and big data analytics. Synapse supports T-SQL-based interaction with ML models and integration with Azure ML endpoints.

3. **Azure Data Factory / Synapse Pipelines**
   Orchestrate the flow of data and automation of model training, scoring, and result delivery.
4. **Data Lake Storage Gen2**
   Acts as a central repository for raw, curated, and trusted data used in training and inference.

---

## Development Lifecycle for ML in Azure

The integration between Azure ML and Synapse follows the ML lifecycle:

1. **Data Preparation** – Curate training data from Synapse SQL or Data Lake.
2. **Model Training** – Use Azure ML workspaces, compute clusters, or automated ML.
3. **Model Registration** – Register trained models in the Azure ML Model Registry.
4. **Deployment** – Expose models as REST endpoints or use Synapse Predict T-SQL function.
5. **Scoring / Inference** – Score batch or streaming data in pipelines.
6. **Monitoring** – Track performance, retrain if needed.

---

## Pattern 1: Predictive Model Scoring in Synapse SQL

Once a model is deployed in Azure ML, it can be invoked from Synapse using **T-SQL PREDICT**() for batch scoring.

**Example Scenario:**

A model that predicts customer churn based on demographics and usage history.

**Model Input:**

- Age, Tenure, ContractType, MonthlyCharges

**Deployment:**

1. Train model in Azure ML.
2. Register and deploy to Azure Kubernetes Service (AKS) or managed endpoint.
3. Connect Synapse to Azure ML workspace.

**Synapse SQL Query:**

```
SELECT
CustomerID,
PREDICT(MODEL = [dbo].[ChurnModel],
DATA =
SELECT Age, Tenure, ContractType, MonthlyCharges
FROM customer_features
) AS ChurnProbability
FROM customer_features;
```

This allows you to embed predictive logic directly within SQL-based workflows or Power BI reports that connect to Synapse.

---

## Pattern 2: Batch Scoring via Data Factory or Synapse Pipelines

In cases where batch processing is preferred or models require complex input features, scoring can be done through pipelines.

**Steps:**

1. ADF extracts data from Synapse or ADLS.
2. Data is passed to Azure ML endpoint using Web Activity or AzureML Execute Pipeline.
3. Inference results are written back to ADLS or Synapse for downstream use.

**Example: Scoring Risk for Loan Applications**

```
{
"method": "POST",
"url": "https://<ml-endpoint>/score",
"headers": {
"Authorization": "Bearer <token>",
"Content-Type": "application/json"
},
"body": {
"data": [
```

{"Age": 45, "Income": 55000, "LoanAmount": 12000}

]

}

}

Store results in a trusted/predictions/ folder and link back into Power BI or Synapse SQL for analytics.

---

## Pattern 3: Training with Synapse Data

Training data often lives in Synapse SQL pools or ADLS. Azure ML supports seamless data access:

- **From ADLS**: Mount directly using ML compute or Databricks.
- **From Synapse**: Use ODBC/JDBC or export data to blob for consumption.

**Sample Python Code:**

```
import pandas as pd

from azureml.core import Dataset

datastore = ws.get_default_datastore()

dataset = Dataset.Tabular.from_delimited_files(path=[(datastore, 'training/churn.csv')])

df = dataset.to_pandas_dataframe()
```

Train model using sklearn or XGBoost, then register:

```
from azureml.core import Model

Model.register(workspace=ws, model_path="outputs/churn_model.pkl", model_name="ChurnModel")
```

## Pattern 4: Real-Time Scoring with Stream Analytics

Real-time scoring can be implemented using Azure Stream Analytics (ASA) + Azure ML:

1. ASA reads from Event Hub or IoT Hub.
2. ASA invokes Azure ML endpoint for each message.
3. Scored results are sent to Power BI or a database.

**Example ASA Function:**

```
WITH ScoredData AS (

SELECT

EventTime,

Input.*,

MLScore(Input.Age, Input.ContractType) AS ChurnRisk

FROM

InputStream

)

SELECT * INTO OutputStream FROM ScoredData;
```

This enables in-the-moment decisioning such as triggering alerts or recommendations.

## Security and Governance

- Use **Managed Identity** to secure Synapse → Azure ML calls.
- Store secrets in **Azure Key Vault**, referenced in ADF or ML pipelines.
- Use **Private Endpoints** for ML inference traffic.
- Apply **network isolation** to ML compute (VNet integration).
- Track lineage using **Azure Purview**, including ML asset registration.

---

## Model Monitoring and Retraining

Azure ML provides built-in monitoring for:

- **Data Drift**: Changes in input features vs. training data.
- **Model Performance**: AUC, precision, recall degradation.
- **Service Health**: Latency, throughput, errors.

Trigger retraining via ADF or ML pipelines when thresholds are exceeded.

**Example: Automated Retraining Triggered Weekly**

1. Time-triggered pipeline extracts latest labeled data.
2. Re-trains and registers new model.
3. Deploys to production endpoint with versioning.

4. Logs metrics and notifies stakeholders.

---

## Best Practices

- **Use Parquet format** for feature stores to reduce I/O.
- **Version datasets and models** using Azure ML Dataset and Model Registry.
- **Separate training and scoring environments.**
- **Enable logging and telemetry** via Application Insights and ML Monitor.
- **Use dev/test/prod ML environments** managed via workspace isolation or MLOps practices.
- **Incorporate explainability (e.g., SHAP)** where ML decisions affect business outcomes.

---

## Use Cases

1. **Patient Readmission Risk** – Predict likelihood of hospital readmission.
2. **Customer Churn** – Identify at-risk customers based on usage patterns.
3. **Fraud Detection** – Score transactions in real time using ensemble models.
4. **Demand Forecasting** – Generate SKU/store-level forecasts daily.
5. **Document Classification** – Tag incoming documents for workflow automation.

Each use case can be implemented with a common pattern: extract → transform → score → act → monitor.

---

## Summary

Integrating Azure Machine Learning with Synapse enables organizations to operationalize AI models within their existing data estate. Whether using T-SQL predictions inside Synapse, scoring in batch through pipelines, or real-time streaming inference, the platform supports a broad range of ML deployment patterns.

With built-in security, governance, and monitoring features, Azure empowers data scientists, engineers, and analysts to collaborate effectively while maintaining control and compliance. In the next section, we'll explore how to prepare and engineer features from raw data for optimal model performance using Azure-native tools and workflows.

# Data Preparation and Feature Engineering

Data preparation and feature engineering are the most critical steps in the machine learning lifecycle. While advanced algorithms and sophisticated models often get the spotlight, it is the quality and structure of input data that determine the ultimate performance of an ML solution. In Azure, services like Azure Synapse Analytics, Azure Data Factory, Azure Databricks, and Azure Machine Learning come together to enable a powerful and flexible environment for preparing data at scale.

This section provides a detailed look at best practices, design patterns, tools, and workflows for cleaning, transforming, and engineering features from raw datasets. We'll explore techniques for handling structured, semi-structured, and unstructured data, and how to build reusable, scalable data prep pipelines within the Azure ecosystem.

---

## Goals of Data Preparation and Feature Engineering

1. **Cleanse** – Remove inconsistencies, missing values, and outliers.
2. **Standardize** – Normalize formats, units, encodings, and schema.
3. **Transform** – Derive new variables, apply domain-specific calculations.
4. **Aggregate** – Summarize data across dimensions and time.
5. **Encode** – Convert categorical data into machine-readable forms.
6. **Impute** – Handle missing data via statistical or model-based methods.
7. **Scale** – Normalize numerical features for model stability.
8. **Join** – Integrate data from multiple sources into a coherent dataset.

---

## Azure Tools for Data Preparation

| Tool / Service | Purpose |
|---|---|
| **Azure Synapse SQL** | Structured data cleaning, joins, aggregations |
| **Azure Data Factory** | ETL orchestration, Mapping Data Flows for no-code prep |
| **Azure Databricks** | Large-scale processing, Spark-powered transformations |
| **Azure Machine Learning Datasets** | Model-ready data access and profiling |
| **Power Query** | Lightweight data shaping (used in Power BI, ML studio) |

## Example Workflow: Customer Churn Dataset

Let's walk through a full prep pipeline for a customer churn dataset sourced from multiple systems:

1. CRM (Azure SQL)
2. Support Ticket System (JSON via API)
3. Usage Metrics (Parquet in ADLS Gen2)

### Step 1: Ingest and Normalize

Use ADF to ingest and standardize schemas:

```
{
"source": {
"type": "AzureSqlSource"
},
```

```
"sink": {
"type": "ParquetSink"
}
}
```

All data is stored in the **curated** zone in Parquet format. ADF Mapping Data Flows normalize field names and types.

## Handling Missing and Inconsistent Data

**Strategy:**

- Drop fields with excessive missing values.
- Impute numeric fields using median or mode.
- Fill forward time-series gaps for telemetry data.

**Pandas Example in Azure ML Notebook:**

```
df['MonthlyCharges'].fillna(df['MonthlyCharges'].median(), inplace=True)

df['PaymentMethod'].fillna('Unknown', inplace=True)
```

Use visualizations and profiling in Azure ML Studio or Databricks to identify outliers.

## Feature Engineering Techniques

### 1. Binning (Bucketing)

Group continuous variables into discrete bins:

```
df['IncomeGroup'] = pd.cut(df['MonthlyIncome'], bins=[0, 3000, 7000, 20000], labels=['Low', 'Medium', 'High'])
```

**2. Interaction Terms**

Capture relationships between features:

```
df['Contract_PaymentInteraction'] = df['ContractType'] + "_" + df['PaymentMethod']
```

**3. Date Features**

Extract temporal dimensions from datetime columns:

```
df['SignupMonth'] = pd.to_datetime(df['SignupDate']).dt.month

df['TenureYears'] = df['TenureDays'] / 365
```

**4. Lag Features (Time Series)**

Create lagged variables for trend analysis:

```
df['Usage_Lag1'] = df['Usage'].shift(1)
```

**5. Rolling Aggregations**

Use windows for smoothing or trend analysis:

```
df['RollingAvg_3Month'] = df['Usage'].rolling(window=3).mean()
```

## Encoding Categorical Variables

### One-Hot Encoding:

Used for nominal variables with few categories:

```
df = pd.get_dummies(df, columns=['ContractType', 'PaymentMethod'])
```

### Label Encoding:

For ordinal categories:

```
from sklearn.preprocessing import LabelEncoder

le = LabelEncoder()

df['ChurnRisk'] = le.fit_transform(df['ChurnRiskCategory'])
```

## Scaling and Normalization

Most ML models benefit from standardized input ranges:

```
from sklearn.preprocessing import StandardScaler

scaler = StandardScaler()

df[['MonthlyCharges', 'Tenure']] = scaler.fit_transform(df[['MonthlyCharges', 'Tenure']])
```

For tree-based models, scaling is often not necessary, but for models like logistic regression, SVM, or neural networks, it's critical.

## Feature Selection

**Techniques:**

- **Correlation Analysis**
- **Recursive Feature Elimination (RFE)**
- **Variance Threshold**
- **Tree-based Feature Importance**

```
from sklearn.ensemble import RandomForestClassifier

model = RandomForestClassifier()

model.fit(X_train, y_train)

feature_importances = pd.Series(model.feature_importances_, index=X_train.columns)
```

Azure ML Studio offers **automated feature selection** as part of its AutoML pipeline.

---

## Storing and Versioning Features

Azure ML supports **Feature Store (preview)** and **registered datasets**:

- Save processed features as versioned datasets.
- Share across ML experiments and pipelines.
- Audit lineage with Azure Purview.

**Register Dataset Example:**

```
from azureml.core import Dataset

Dataset.Tabular.register_pandas_dataframe(df, target=datastore, name="CustomerChurnFeatures")
```

## Integration with Synapse and Data Lake

Use **serverless SQL pools** to prep features directly in the lake:

```
SELECT

CustomerID,

DATEDIFF(day, SignupDate, GETDATE()) AS Tenure,

CASE

WHEN MonthlyCharges > 100 THEN 'High'

WHEN MonthlyCharges BETWEEN 50 AND 100 THEN 'Medium'

ELSE 'Low'

END AS SpendCategory

FROM

OPENROWSET(

BULK 'https://datalake/curated/customers/*.parquet',

FORMAT='PARQUET'

) AS customers
```

Output to trusted zone for ML consumption.

## Automation with Pipelines

- Use **ADF Pipelines** or **Azure ML Pipelines** to automate:
    - Daily data refresh
    - Re-engineering of features
    - Batch scoring
- Schedule jobs to run in parallel for large datasets.

---

## Best Practices

- Keep transformations **idempotent** and **reproducible**.
- Avoid **data leakage** by ensuring future data isn't used for training.
- Profile data regularly to detect drift.
- Document all transformations in code or metadata.
- Use **unit tests** and **data validation frameworks** like Great Expectations.

---

## Summary

Feature engineering is a blend of domain knowledge, statistical insight, and data engineering. In Azure, the convergence of tools like Data Factory, Synapse, Databricks, and Azure ML enables practitioners to build robust pipelines that prepare data for machine learning at enterprise scale.

By focusing on clean, well-engineered, and versioned features, organizations not only improve model performance but also lay the foundation for reproducibility, compliance, and collaboration in AI initiatives. In the next section, we'll cover how to deploy these models within Synapse Workspaces for seamless, integrated model serving.

# Deploying Models within Synapse Workspaces

After training and fine-tuning a machine learning model, deployment is the next critical step. Deployment allows models to serve real-world inference requests—whether for batch scoring large datasets, enabling real-time predictions in applications, or integrating outputs into business intelligence platforms like Power BI.

Azure Synapse Analytics provides native support for deploying and operationalizing models within its unified workspace. This allows for seamless integration between data preparation, training, deployment, and scoring—all within a single environment. In this section, we'll explore how to deploy models in Synapse Workspaces, using both traditional deployment endpoints and embedded scoring methods like PREDICT in T-SQL. We'll cover architectural patterns, deployment options, pipeline integration, and performance optimization.

---

## Deployment Options in Synapse Workspaces

There are multiple ways to operationalize machine learning models in Synapse:

1. **T-SQL PREDICT Statement**

2. **Azure ML Endpoint Integration via External Services**
3. **Apache Spark Pools with MLflow**
4. **Batch Scoring with Synapse Pipelines**

Each option suits different use cases depending on latency, volume, and model complexity.

---

## Option 1: T-SQL PREDICT with ONNX Models

Synapse allows ONNX (Open Neural Network Exchange) models to be invoked directly from T-SQL using the PREDICT function. This is ideal for in-database scoring.

**Step-by-Step:**

1. Train a model using Azure ML, convert to ONNX.
2. Register the ONNX model in Synapse.
3. Use PREDICT to apply it to your dataset.

**Example: Churn Prediction Using ONNX**

```
CREATE MODEL [dbo].[ChurnModel]

FROM (SELECT * FROM dbo.customer_features)

WITH (MODEL = 'https://<storageaccount>.blob.core.windows.net/models/churn.onnx');

SELECT

CustomerID,

PREDICT(MODEL = dbo.ChurnModel,
```

```
DATA = SELECT Age, Tenure, MonthlyCharges FROM dbo.customer_features
) AS ChurnProbability
FROM dbo.customer_features;
```

**Benefits:**

- No need for external API calls.
- Low latency for batch or interactive scoring.
- Integrated with Synapse SQL pools.

---

## Option 2: Azure ML Endpoint Integration

For models too complex to run in-database (e.g., deep learning), use Azure Machine Learning to deploy a model as a REST API and call it from Synapse Pipelines or Notebooks.

**Deployment via Azure ML:**

```
from azureml.core import Model
from azureml.core.webservice import AciWebservice, Webservice
deployment_config = AciWebservice.deploy_configuration(cpu_cores=1, memory_gb=1)
service = Model.deploy(workspace=ws,
name='loan-default-predictor',
models=[model],
```

```
inference_config=inference_config,
deployment_config=deployment_config)
service.wait_for_deployment(show_output=True)
```

**Invocation from Synapse Notebook:**

```
import requests
import json
scoring_uri = 'https://<your-service>.azurewebsites.net/score'
input_data = json.dumps({"data": [[42, "Male", 50000, 3]]})
headers = {'Content-Type': 'application/json'}
response = requests.post(scoring_uri, input_data, headers=headers)
print(response.json())
```

**Invocation from Synapse Pipeline (Web Activity):**

```
{
"type": "WebActivity",
"name": "CallMLScoringAPI",
"dependsOn": [],
"policy": {},
"typeProperties": {
"url": "https://<endpoint>/score",
```

```
"method": "POST",
"headers": {
"Content-Type": "application/json"
},
"body": "{\"data\": [{\"feature1\": 10, \"feature2\": 25}]}"
}
}
```

---

## Option 3: Spark Pools with MLflow in Synapse

Apache Spark in Synapse provides a flexible environment for deploying and managing models using MLflow.

**MLflow Deployment Workflow:**

1. Train model in Synapse Spark using Scikit-learn, PySpark, or other supported libraries.
2. Log and register the model with MLflow.
3. Load the model and perform batch scoring on DataFrames.

```
import mlflow.sklearn

model_uri = "models:/LoanDefaultModel/1"

model = mlflow.sklearn.load_model(model_uri)

df = spark.read.parquet("abfss://trusted@datalake.dfs.core.windows.net/loan_applications")

pandas_df = df.toPandas()
```

predictions = model.predict(pandas_df)

**Advantages:**

- Supports complex models.
- Easily scaled via Spark.
- Full integration with Synapse Workspaces.

---

## Option 4: Batch Scoring via Synapse Pipelines

For large datasets that need periodic scoring, use Synapse Pipelines with SQL or Spark activities to automate the process.

**Batch Scoring Steps:**

1. Ingest new data via ADF/ADF-embedded Synapse pipeline.
2. Use a Notebook activity to apply the model to the dataset.
3. Store results in trusted zone or publish to Power BI.

**Notebook Scoring Cell Example:**

df_new = spark.read.parquet("abfss://curated@datalake.dfs.core.windows.net/new_customers/")

preds = model.predict(df_new.toPandas())

result_df = spark.createDataFrame(preds)

result_df.write.parquet("abfss://trusted@datalake.dfs.core.windows.net/churn_predictions/")

**Trigger Mechanisms:**

- Time-based (e.g., daily at 1 AM).
- Event-based (e.g., new file arrives).
- Manual trigger via Synapse Studio.

---

## Logging and Monitoring

Proper logging is vital for production-grade ML deployments.

- Use **Application Insights** with Azure ML for model telemetry.
- Track predictions, latency, and exceptions.
- Use **Azure Monitor** and **Log Analytics** to consolidate metrics.

**ML Monitoring Metrics:**

- Prediction confidence distribution
- Input feature drift
- Model response times
- Versioning and rollback history

---

## Security and Governance

Ensure deployments comply with enterprise security policies:

- Use **Azure Private Endpoints** for secure inference traffic.
- Enable **Role-Based Access Control (RBAC)** on Synapse and ML workspaces.
- Store API secrets and tokens in **Azure Key Vault**.
- Use **Purview** to trace model input and output lineage.

---

## Best Practices

1. **Use T-SQL PREDICT for simple models** that require tight integration with SQL-based tools.
2. **Deploy via Azure ML endpoints** when serving complex or black-box models.
3. **Leverage Spark with MLflow** for high-scale batch or parallel workloads.
4. **Isolate dev, test, and prod models** via separate endpoints or workspace registration.
5. **Document models thoroughly**—input schema, version, author, performance metrics.
6. **Use Data Drift Detectors** and schedule retraining as necessary.
7. **Monitor scoring pipelines** to detect failures and latency spikes.

---

## Use Cases

1. **Marketing** – Batch score leads weekly to prioritize sales outreach.
2. **Finance** – Score loans nightly based on latest risk factors.

3. **Healthcare** – Real-time scoring for ER triage via API.
4. **Retail** – Predict product affinity and customer churn within Power BI.
5. **Manufacturing** – Daily asset failure risk scoring fed into operations dashboard.

Each use case benefits from different deployment methods, showcasing the flexibility of Synapse Workspaces for enterprise-scale ML deployment.

---

## Summary

Deploying models within Synapse Workspaces enables organizations to embed machine learning seamlessly into their analytics ecosystem. Whether you're scoring millions of rows via SQL or serving real-time inferences via APIs, Synapse offers the tools and integrations to operationalize ML effectively.

From low-latency batch scoring to complex deep learning services, deployment strategies can be tailored to fit the performance, cost, and compliance needs of your business. The final piece of the puzzle is maintaining and monitoring these models in production, which we'll cover in the next section focused on model lifecycle management and monitoring.

# Model Monitoring and Maintenance

Successfully deploying a machine learning model into production is only part of the machine learning lifecycle. Once a model is live, it becomes a dynamic component of a larger system—subject to changing data distributions, evolving user behaviors, regulatory requirements, and infrastructure constraints. To ensure continued accuracy, reliability, and compliance, organizations must implement rigorous **model monitoring** and **maintenance** practices.

In Azure, model lifecycle management can be seamlessly integrated using Azure Machine Learning (Azure ML), Azure Monitor, Application Insights, Synapse Pipelines, and supporting services. This section explores best practices and practical techniques for monitoring ML models, detecting drift and degradation, automating retraining workflows, and managing versioned deployments to ensure sustained business value.

---

## Objectives of Model Monitoring

1. **Performance Monitoring**

   ○ Track prediction accuracy, precision, recall, and F1-score.

   ○ Compare real-time predictions with ground truth when available.

2. **Data Drift Detection**

   ○ Detect changes in the statistical properties of input features and prediction distributions.

3. **Model Decay Management**

   ○ Identify when a model's performance deteriorates due to changing patterns or external influences.

4. **Resource and Service Health Monitoring**

   ○ Ensure deployed endpoints are healthy and responsive.

5. **Audit and Compliance Logging**

○ Capture all inference calls, version usage, and data lineage for regulatory purposes.

---

## Tools for Monitoring in Azure

| Tool / Service | Functionality |
|---|---|
| **Azure ML Monitoring** | Native logging of predictions, inputs, outputs |
| **Application Insights** | Telemetry and tracing for deployed services |
| **Azure Monitor** | Aggregated metrics and alerting |
| **Log Analytics** | Centralized queryable logs and metrics |
| **Synapse Pipelines** | Operational orchestration and conditional logic |
| **Azure Purview** | Lineage tracking and sensitivity labeling |

## Logging and Telemetry with Application Insights

Azure ML can integrate with Application Insights to log detailed telemetry of deployed web services.

**Logged Items Include:**

- Request timestamps
- Payload size
- Input and output schema
- Inference latency
- Error messages

- Status codes

**Python Example – Logging Custom Events:**

```
from applicationinsights import TelemetryClient

tc = TelemetryClient('<instrumentation_key>')

tc.track_event('InferenceComplete', {'model_version': 'v2', 'result': 'churn=0'})

tc.flush()
```

Use Azure Monitor Alerts on:

- Average response time exceeding 500ms
- HTTP 500 errors > threshold
- Consecutive timeouts

---

## Model Performance Monitoring

When ground truth labels are available, implement a feedback loop to calculate post-deployment metrics.

**Step-by-Step:**

1. Log predictions with request metadata (user ID, timestamp, features).
2. Collect actual outcomes in a separate pipeline (e.g., churn/no churn, default/no default).
3. Join prediction and outcome on ID and time.
4. Recalculate confusion matrix, precision, recall, etc.

**Metrics Computation Example (SQL):**

```
SELECT

COUNT(*) AS Total,

SUM(CASE WHEN Actual = 1 AND Predicted = 1 THEN 1 ELSE 0 END) AS TP,

SUM(CASE WHEN Actual = 0 AND Predicted = 1 THEN 1 ELSE 0 END) AS FP,

SUM(CASE WHEN Actual = 1 AND Predicted = 0 THEN 1 ELSE 0 END) AS FN

FROM scored_predictions

JOIN actual_outcomes ON scored_predictions.ID = actual_outcomes.ID;
```

Automate this process weekly or monthly to detect performance drop.

---

## Data Drift Detection

Data drift can be structural (feature distributions change) or behavioral (target distribution or prediction rate changes).

Azure ML supports drift detection between:

- Training data vs inference data
- Inference data over time

**Setting Up Drift Monitor:**

1. Register baseline dataset in Azure ML.

2. Create monitoring schedule comparing baseline and production data.
3. Define thresholds for acceptable variation (e.g., Kullback-Leibler divergence or PSI).
4. Trigger retraining or alerts on threshold breach.

**Drift Detection Code Snippet:**

```
from azureml.datadrift import DataDriftDetector

monitor = DataDriftDetector.create_from_datasets(

workspace=ws,

name='churn-monitor',

baseline_data_set=baseline_ds,

target_data_set=production_ds,

features=['Age', 'Tenure', 'MonthlyCharges'],

compute_target='cpu-cluster',

frequency='Week'

)

monitor.start()
```

## Automated Retraining Pipelines

Retraining ensures models remain accurate as new data arrives or behavior changes.

**Pipeline Components:**

1. **Trigger**: Time-based (weekly) or event-based (drift detected).
2. **Retrain**: Load latest labeled data, engineer features, train model.
3. **Evaluate**: Compare with previous model on hold-out set.
4. **Register**: Version and store the new model.
5. **Deploy**: Replace production model if performance improves.
6. **Notify**: Send alerts if retraining fails or performance drops.

**Azure ML Pipeline Example:**

```
from azureml.pipeline.core import Pipeline

pipeline = Pipeline(workspace=ws, steps=[data_prep_step, train_step, evaluate_step, register_step])

pipeline.validate()

pipeline.submit("weekly_retraining_pipeline")
```

Trigger this via ADF or Synapse Pipeline weekly, or on-demand.

## Model Versioning and Lifecycle

Use Azure ML's model registry to track versions.

| Version | Accuracy | Created Date | Notes |
|---|---|---|---|
| v1 | 0.82 | 2024-10-01 | Initial model |
| v2 | 0.86 | 2024-12-15 | Retrained |
| v3 | 0.79 | 2025-03-01 | Lower accuracy |

**Best Practices:**

- Always tag models with metadata (dataset, algorithm, parameters).
- Use champion-challenger approach: keep prior model until new one is validated.
- Implement rollback logic in deployment pipelines.

**Versioned Inference Example:**

```
model = Model(ws, name="LoanDefaultModel", version=2)
```

## Governance and Compliance

Monitoring is also essential for compliance with regulations like HIPAA, GDPR, and AI-specific laws (e.g., EU AI Act).

- Log all access to models.
- Store and encrypt scoring logs for 7+ years.
- Use Azure Purview to link predictions to source datasets.
- Implement model cards: documentation describing model purpose, risks, and fairness.

**Model Card Metadata:**

- Intended Use: "Predict customer churn"
- Training Dataset: 2023 CRM records
- Bias Assessment: None detected across age or gender

- Approval Date: 2024-11-01
- Responsible Team: Data Science

---

## Best Practices

1. **Monitor both predictions and service health.**
2. **Automate retraining but review manually before deploying.**
3. **Visualize drift trends in Power BI for transparency.**
4. **Alert early to prevent model decay.**
5. **Keep a historical audit trail of predictions and versions.**
6. **Use explainability tools (e.g., SHAP) in monitoring dashboards.**

---

## Summary

Machine learning models are not static assets—they are living entities that must evolve with the data and the environment in which they operate. In Azure, comprehensive monitoring and maintenance capabilities empower teams to ensure sustained model performance, regulatory compliance, and operational excellence.

From logging predictions and detecting drift to automating retraining and managing model lifecycles, the Azure ML ecosystem provides all the tools necessary to build resilient, self-healing ML systems. By embedding monitoring into the core of your ML strategy, you safeguard both the technical integrity and business value of your AI investments.

# Chapter 9: Governance, Security, and Best Practices

## Role-Based Access Control and Policies

Role-Based Access Control (RBAC) is a cornerstone of secure, scalable Azure architectures. It enables fine-grained management of permissions across resources by assigning roles to users, groups, service principals, and managed identities. When used alongside data-specific access control systems such as Azure Data Lake Access Control Lists (ACLs), SQL security roles, and policy enforcement frameworks, RBAC provides a consistent and auditable approach to protecting data and resources.

In a modern data platform, especially in industries subject to regulatory compliance (e.g., healthcare, finance, government), it is essential to control **who can do what, where, and when.** This section explores how to implement RBAC in Azure, integrate it with data services, design secure access models, and ensure policy-driven governance across the platform.

---

### What is Role-Based Access Control?

RBAC in Azure defines access to resources using the following elements:

- **Security Principal**: A user, group, service principal, or managed identity that needs access.
- **Role Definition**: A collection of permissions that define what actions can be performed (e.g., Reader, Contributor, Owner, or custom roles).

- **Scope**: The boundary of access — subscription, resource group, or individual resource.

**RBAC Decision Logic:**

1. Determine who the user is.
2. Evaluate what roles the user has.
3. Determine whether those roles grant permissions to the resource at the given scope.

---

## Built-in vs Custom Roles

Azure provides over 70 built-in roles, but you can also create custom roles for more granular access.

**Common Built-in Roles:**

- **Reader**: Can view everything but cannot make changes.

- **Contributor**: Can make changes but cannot grant access.

- **Owner**: Full access, including granting access to others.

- **Storage Blob Data Reader**: Grants read access to blob data.

- **Synapse Administrator**: Full control over Synapse workspaces.

**Custom Role Definition Example:**

```
{
"Name": "DataLake Curated Zone Reader",
"Description": "Read-only access to curated datasets in ADLS",
"Actions": [
"Microsoft.Storage/storageAccounts/read",
"Microsoft.Storage/storageAccounts/blobServices/containers/blobs/read"
],
"NotActions": [],
"AssignableScopes": ["/subscriptions/xxxx/resourceGroups/data-rg"]
}
```

## Assigning Roles in Azure

Roles can be assigned using the Azure Portal, Azure CLI, PowerShell, or ARM templates.

**Azure CLI Example:**

```
az role assignment create \
—assignee "<user@domain.com>" \
—role "Storage Blob Data Reader" \
```

—scope "/subscriptions/<sub-id>/resourceGroups/data-rg/providers/Microsoft.Storage/storageAccounts/mydatalake"

Use **least privilege principle**: assign the lowest level of permissions needed for the task.

---

## RBAC in Data Services

### Azure Data Lake Storage Gen2

- Uses **Azure RBAC** for container-level permissions.
- Supports **POSIX-style ACLs** for file/folder-level access.

**Best Practice:** Combine RBAC for resource-level control and ACLs for granular access within the filesystem.

**Set ACLs Example (CLI):**

az storage fs access set \

—path "trusted/sales" \

—acl "user:<objectId>:r-x" \

—account-name mydatalake \

—file-system myfilesystem

### Synapse Analytics

- Permissions managed via **SQL security model** and **Synapse RBAC roles.**

- Supports **object-level security** (OLS) and **row-level security** (RLS).

**Example: Granting SQL Read Access to a Role:**

```
CREATE ROLE data_analyst;

GRANT SELECT ON SCHEMA::sales TO data_analyst;

EXEC sp_addrolemember 'data_analyst', 'user@domain.com';
```

**Power BI**

- Uses **workspace roles**: Admin, Member, Contributor, Viewer.
- Integrates with **Azure AD groups** for managing access at scale.

**Tip:** Use **Power BI Security Groups** in Azure AD and automate membership via Identity Governance.

---

## Governance with Azure Policy

Azure Policy enforces organizational standards by creating **guardrails** for resource deployment and management.

**Common Policies:**

- Require tags on all resources.
- Restrict location of resource deployments.
- Enforce use of managed identity.

- Audit unencrypted storage accounts.

**Policy Assignment Example (CLI):**

```
az policy assignment create \

—name "enforce-tagging" \

—policy "/providers/Microsoft.Authorization/policyDefinitions/enforce-tagging" \

—scope "/subscriptions/<sub-id>/resourceGroups/data-rg"
```

**Best Practice:** Combine **Azure Policy** with **Blueprints** to govern larger sets of resources.

---

## Data Access Scenarios

**Scenario 1: Business Analysts Accessing Curated Data**

- Assign Storage Blob Data Reader at the container level.
- Set ACLs to allow read access only to /curated/ subfolders.
- Use RLS in Synapse for sensitive columns.

**Scenario 2: ML Engineers Running Training Jobs**

- Assign Contributor role to Azure ML workspace.
- Use managed identity to access ADLS, Synapse.
- Restrict access to only the training datasets.

**Scenario 3: External Consultants Needing Temporary Access**

- Assign temporary access using **PIM (Privileged Identity Management)**.
- Set access review schedules.
- Use scoped RBAC and restrict API access via Key Vault.

---

## Audit and Logging

To ensure accountability and visibility:

- Enable **Activity Logs** in Azure Monitor.
- Use **Log Analytics Workspace** for centralized queries.
- Enable **Azure Storage Diagnostics** and **Synapse Auditing.**
- Connect to **Microsoft Sentinel** for security analytics.

**Query Example – Users Accessing Sensitive Folder:**

```
StorageBlobLogs
| where Uri contains "trusted/patient_data"
| project TimeGenerated, Uri, AuthenticationType, OperationName, CallerIpAddress, Identity
```

---

## Least Privilege and Zero Trust Principles

1. **Minimize access duration**: Use time-bound assignments

(e.g., PIM).

2. **Monitor usage**: Regularly audit access logs.
3. **Automate revocation**: Remove access when projects or contracts end.
4. **Segregate duties**: Separate data engineering from model scoring and BI access.
5. **Use conditional access**: Require MFA, restrict by device or location.

---

## Automation and Infrastructure as Code

RBAC and policy configurations should be included in IaC practices.

**ARM/Bicep Role Assignment Snippet:**

```
resource roleAssignment 'Microsoft.Authorization/roleAssignments@2020-04-01-preview' = {

name: guid(subscription().id, userPrincipalId, roleDefinitionId)

properties: {

principalId: userPrincipalId

roleDefinitionId: roleDefinitionResource.id

scope: storageAccount.id

}

}
```

**Tip:** Store access definitions in GitHub or ADO repos with review workflows.

## Summary

Implementing Role-Based Access Control and policy governance in Azure is fundamental to managing access, ensuring data security, and achieving compliance. With native integration across data services—Synapse, ADLS, ML, and Power BI—Azure provides a unified model for defining, assigning, and auditing permissions.

Organizations should embrace RBAC not just as a security control, but as a tool for collaboration, clarity, and accountability in their data strategy. Paired with Azure Policy, Activity Logs, and automated deployment strategies, RBAC ensures that access is always controlled, appropriate, and traceable.

In the next section, we'll explore how auditing and threat detection further enhance the trust and security posture of your Azure data environment.

# Auditing and Threat Detection

In an era where data is both a critical asset and a primary target, robust auditing and threat detection mechanisms are essential for maintaining trust, compliance, and operational integrity. Azure provides a comprehensive suite of tools to audit activity, detect threats in real time, and respond effectively to potential security incidents across your data estate.

This section covers how to implement end-to-end auditing and threat detection in Azure with a focus on data services such as Azure Data Lake, Azure SQL, Synapse Analytics, Azure Storage, and Power BI. We'll also explore integrations with Microsoft Defender for Cloud, Azure Monitor, and Microsoft Sentinel to provide a layered defense-in-depth strategy.

## Objectives of Auditing and Threat Detection

1. **Monitor Data Access and Usage**

○ Track who accessed what, when, from where, and how.

2. **Identify and Investigate Anomalies**

○ Detect suspicious behavior such as data exfiltration, privilege escalation, or brute-force access attempts.

3. **Support Regulatory Compliance**

○ Provide evidence for GDPR, HIPAA, SOX, and ISO 27001 requirements.

4. **Enable Incident Response**

○ Integrate alerts into security operations workflows and automate remediation.

---

## Azure Tools for Auditing and Threat Detection

| Tool / Service | Purpose |
|---|---|
| **Azure Activity Logs** | Audit management operations at the control plane |
| **Azure Monitor** | Aggregate logs and metrics, support alerts |
| **Log Analytics** | Central log query engine (Kusto Query Language) |
| **Microsoft Defender for Cloud** | Real-time threat detection for Azure services |
| **Microsoft Sentinel** | SIEM for log correlation, investigation, and response |
| **Azure Storage Diagnostics** | Access logs for blobs and files |
| **SQL and Synapse Auditing** | Record and archive all query and access activity |
| **Power BI Audit Logs** | Log report usage, data access, and user interactions |

## Control Plane vs Data Plane

- **Control Plane** logs capture management operations (e.g., creating or deleting resources).
- **Data Plane** logs capture operations on the data itself (e.g., reading, writing, deleting files or rows).

Both planes must be monitored for a complete picture.

## Setting Up Activity Logs

Azure automatically retains Activity Logs for 90 days. To persist them, export logs to:

- **Azure Storage Account** (long-term archive)
- **Event Hub** (streaming to external SIEMs)
- **Log Analytics Workspace** (for query and alerting)

**CLI Example: Export Activity Logs to Log Analytics**

```
az monitor log-profiles create \
—name "activity-log-export" \
—locations "global" \
—categories "Write" "Delete" "Action" \
—retention 365 \
—workspace-id "/subscriptions/.../resourcegroups/rg/providers/microsoft.operationalinsights/workspaces/myLogAnalytics"
```

## Auditing in Synapse Analytics

Synapse supports **SQL auditing** and **workspace-level diagnostics**:

1. **SQL Pool Auditing**

    ○ Capture successful/failed logins, executed queries, permission changes.

    ○ Output to Log Analytics, Event Hubs, or Storage.

2. **Workspace Diagnostics**

   ○ Track notebook usage, pipeline runs, Spark job submissions.

**Enable Auditing (Portal):**

- Go to Synapse workspace > Auditing > Enable.
- Choose destination (e.g., Log Analytics).

**Query Example: List All Login Attempts**

```
AzureDiagnostics
| where Category == "SQLSecurityAuditEvents"
| where action_name_s contains "login"
| project TimeGenerated, session_id_s, database_name_s, server_principal_name_s, succeeded_s
```

---

## Threat Detection with Defender for SQL and Synapse

**Microsoft Defender for SQL** provides:

- Brute force attack detection
- SQL injection detection
- Anomalous access patterns
- Suspicious admin operations

**Configuration:**

- Enable at the server or Synapse workspace level.
- Alerts sent via email, Event Grid, or integrated with Sentinel.

**Sample Alert:**

- "Potential SQL injection attempt detected from IP 192.0.2.10"

Integrate with automated response workflows for rapid mitigation.

## Monitoring Azure Data Lake and Blob Storage

Use **Storage Diagnostics** to enable logs for read, write, and delete events.

**Enable via CLI:**

```
az storage logging update \
—account-name mystorageacct \
—log rwd \
—retention 30 \
—services b \
—container-logging true
```

**Log Schema Includes:**

- Operation type (e.g., GetBlob, PutBlob)
- Requestor IP

- Authentication method
- URI and container

**Common Detection Patterns:**

- High download volume in short time
- Access from unfamiliar geolocations
- Anonymous or SAS-token usage

---

## Power BI Audit Logs

Audit logs track:

- Report views
- Dataset refreshes
- Sharing events
- DLP policy violations

Access via Microsoft 365 compliance portal or use the **Power BI Admin API** to extract logs into Azure Data Explorer or Sentinel.

**Automated Extraction with PowerShell:**

```
Search-UnifiedAuditLog -StartDate (Get-Date).AddDays(-1) -EndDate (Get-Date) -Operations "ViewedReport"
```

## Microsoft Sentinel Integration

Sentinel acts as a centralized security information and event management (SIEM) system.

**Capabilities:**

- Ingest logs from Synapse, SQL, Storage, Power BI
- Run playbooks for incident response (e.g., revoke access, notify SOC)
- Visualize attacks using investigation graphs

**Example Analytics Rule:**

- Trigger alert when >500 rows accessed from ADLS in <60 seconds by the same identity.

**Playbook Example:**

- On alert:
  - Suspend user account.
  - Notify admin via Teams.
  - Archive logs.

---

## Custom Threat Detection Logic

Use **Kusto Query Language (KQL)** in Log Analytics or Sentinel to create custom detections.

**Detect Large Data Downloads from Synapse**

```
AzureDiagnostics
| where Category == "SQLSecurityAuditEvents"
| where action_name_s == "SELECT"
| summarize RowCount=sum(row_count_d) by bin(TimeGenerated, 10m), client_ip_s
| where RowCount > 100000
```

---

## Incident Response and Remediation

Steps for handling data security incidents:

1. **Detect** via alerts or dashboards.
2. **Investigate** using full logs and historical access data.
3. **Contain** by revoking access or disabling identities.
4. **Remediate** by patching systems or updating policies.
5. **Review** the incident and document findings.
6. **Automate** similar responses in the future.

---

## Best Practices

- **Centralize logs**: Use Log Analytics for all services.
- **Enable Defender for Cloud**: Baseline protection and alerts.
- **Ingest into Sentinel**: For correlation and automated response.

- **Review logs regularly**: Build dashboards for key indicators.
- **Implement DLP policies**: Prevent unauthorized data sharing in Power BI and M365.
- **Conduct security audits**: At least quarterly.

---

### Summary

Auditing and threat detection are critical components of a secure and compliant data platform. Azure's native tools—ranging from Activity Logs and SQL Auditing to Microsoft Defender and Sentinel—provide deep visibility into every action and potential risk within your data environment.

By proactively monitoring for threats, automating responses, and maintaining detailed audit trails, organizations can ensure they meet compliance mandates, protect sensitive data, and build trust in their data-driven operations. The next section explores how to catalog, classify, and trace data using Azure Purview to further strengthen your governance posture.

## Data Cataloging and Lineage with Purview

As modern data platforms scale to ingest, process, and serve information across hundreds of sources and consumers, maintaining control and visibility becomes increasingly complex. Data consumers often struggle to find, understand, and trust the datasets they need, while data stewards grapple with questions of compliance, ownership, and security. Azure Purview—a unified data governance solution—addresses this challenge by delivering enterprise-grade

**data cataloging**, **lineage tracking**, **classification**, and **insight visualization**.

In this section, we'll explore how to use Azure Purview to build a centralized data catalog, automatically scan and classify data assets, understand data lineage across services, and provide secure, searchable access for all stakeholders. By the end, you'll understand how to establish a metadata-driven governance framework that enhances collaboration, trust, and compliance across your Azure data estate.

---

## What Is Azure Purview?

Azure Purview is a cloud-native data governance platform that provides:

- **Automated data discovery** from a wide range of on-prem and cloud sources.
- **Data cataloging** with business and technical metadata.
- **Data classification** with built-in and custom classifiers.
- **End-to-end data lineage** across data movement and transformation.
- **Role-based access** for managing visibility and collaboration.

Purview helps answer critical questions:

- What data do we have?
- Where did it come from?

- Who owns it?
- How is it classified?
- Who is using it, and how?

---

## Architecture and Components

| Component | Description |
|---|---|
| Purview Account | Central entry point for governance activities |
| Scan Ruleset | Defines how metadata is extracted during scans |
| Data Map | Graph of discovered metadata and relationships |
| Catalog | Searchable interface for data discovery |
| Insights | Reports on sensitive data, asset activity, and data usage |
| Lineage View | Visualization of data flow across systems |
| Classification Rules | Custom logic for detecting sensitive or structured data types |

Purview integrates with Azure services such as Synapse, Data Factory, SQL, Blob Storage, Power BI, and non-Azure sources like Amazon S3, SAP, Oracle, and more.

---

## Setting Up Azure Purview

### Step 1: Create a Purview Account

```
az purview account create \
—name myPurviewAccount \
—resource-group rg-data-governance \
```

—location eastus

**Step 2: Assign Data Reader Role**

Ensure the Purview managed identity has read access to your data sources (e.g., Storage Blob Data Reader for ADLS).

---

## Registering and Scanning Data Sources

You must register data sources in Purview and configure scan rulesets.

**Example: Registering an ADLS Gen2 Account**

- Go to Purview Studio → Sources → Register.
- Select **Azure Data Lake Storage Gen2**.
- Enter storage account name and scan scope (container/ path).
- Assign permissions to Purview managed identity.

**Scan Configuration:**

- Schedule scans (daily/weekly).
- Choose built-in classifiers (email, credit card, DOB).
- Select metadata extraction (schema, statistics, classifications).

---

## Metadata Enrichment and Stewardship

Once assets are discovered, you can enrich them with business metadata:

- **Glossary Terms**: Define domain-specific concepts (e.g., "Customer", "Policy Number").
- **Asset Owners**: Assign responsible data stewards or teams.
- **Descriptions and Tags**: Add clarity to column meanings and dataset purpose.
- **Classifications**: Automatically or manually label fields (e.g., "PII", "Financial Data").

**Example: Adding a Glossary Term via UI**

- Navigate to Glossary → + Add Term
- Term: CustomerSegment
- Definition: Grouping of customers based on purchase behavior
- Assign term to relevant datasets or columns

---

## Data Lineage and Impact Analysis

Lineage provides a visual graph showing how data flows from source to destination.

**Automatic Lineage Sources:**

- **Azure Data Factory Pipelines**
- **Azure Synapse Pipelines and Notebooks**
- **Power BI Datasets**
- **SQL stored procedures (to some extent)**

**Use Case: Tracing a Report in Power BI**

1. Power BI dashboard is connected to a Synapse view.
2. The Synapse view pulls from a table populated by a Data Factory pipeline.
3. That pipeline ingests CSV files from ADLS Gen2.

Purview visualizes the entire chain, enabling:

- **Impact analysis**: Understand which reports are affected by upstream schema changes.
- **Root cause tracing**: Identify source changes behind data quality issues.
- **Compliance verification**: Confirm that regulated data has appropriate transformations and masking.

---

## Custom Classification and Sensitivity Labels

Azure Purview includes over 100 built-in classifiers (e.g., email, credit card number, national ID), but you can also create custom rules.

**Example: Custom Regex Classifier for IBAN**

```
{
"name": "IBANClassifier",
"type": "Regex",
"pattern":
"[A-Z]{2}[0-9]{2}[A-Z0-9]{4}[0-9]{7}([A-Z0-9]?){0,16}"
}
```

Assign classifications at the column level or propagate them from upstream sources.

---

## Access and Collaboration

Data stewards, analysts, engineers, and auditors can access the catalog based on their roles.

- **Search and browse** using keywords, tags, or glossary terms.
- **Filter** by classification, owner, domain, or sensitivity level.
- **Request access** to datasets through integrated workflows (preview).

**Tip:** Use **Azure AD groups** to manage catalog visibility and enable separation by department or data domain.

---

## Reporting and Insights

Purview provides built-in insights dashboards, including:

- **Sensitive Data Insights**: What PII/PHI exists and where.
- **Scan Status Dashboard**: Coverage across sources.
- **Ownership Overview**: Number of assets without owners.
- **Classification Coverage**: Percentage of classified assets.

Use these to:

- Prioritize data stewardship activities.
- Track data governance progress.
- Identify areas of risk or neglect.

---

## Automation and API Integration

Purview supports REST APIs and SDKs to automate tasks:

- Programmatically register sources.
- Trigger scans on-demand.
- Import/export glossary terms.
- Integrate with DevOps workflows.

**Example: Trigger a Scan via API**

POST /scan/jobs

```
{
"scanLevel": "Full",
"scanRuleSetName": "DefaultRuleSet",
"resourceId": "/subscriptions/.../resourceGroups/.../providers/Microsoft.Storage/storageAccounts/mydatalake"
}
```

Use in CI/CD pipelines to ensure new assets are scanned and cataloged post-deployment.

---

## Integration with Microsoft Information Protection (MIP)

Purview can recognize **Microsoft Sensitivity Labels** and propagate them across services. This enables:

- Consistent classification across M365 and Azure.
- DLP policy enforcement in Power BI.
- Label-based access control (e.g., "Highly Confidential" blocks external sharing).

---

## Best Practices

1. **Automate scans** to keep metadata current.
2. **Use glossary terms** to bridge business and technical users.
3. **Assign data owners** for all critical datasets.
4. **Monitor lineage** regularly to detect breaks or manual updates.
5. **Limit metadata sprawl** by applying rulesets to only

required datasets.

6. **Establish governance committees** to review classification and lineage policies.

---

## Summary

Azure Purview transforms data governance from a manual, ad-hoc process into an automated, scalable, and user-friendly system. By cataloging, classifying, and visualizing your data estate, it provides both technical and business stakeholders with the tools to find, understand, and trust data.

Whether you're enabling self-service analytics, ensuring regulatory compliance, or managing complex transformation pipelines, Purview offers the visibility and control required to drive your data platform forward with confidence. In the next section, we'll turn to cost optimization and resource management strategies to ensure your Azure data solutions remain sustainable and efficient.

# Cost Control and Resource Management

Operating at scale in the cloud comes with immense power and flexibility—but also the potential for spiraling costs if not carefully managed. As data platforms grow more complex, with services like Azure Synapse Analytics, Azure Data Lake Storage Gen2, Azure SQL, Azure Machine Learning, and Data Factory all working together, maintaining cost efficiency requires proactive governance, observability, and optimization strategies.

This section presents an in-depth guide to managing costs and optimizing resource utilization across Azure's data ecosystem. From budgeting and tagging to right-sizing compute and analyzing usage patterns, we'll walk through practical techniques and tools to help you ensure that your cloud investments deliver maximum business value without unnecessary expense.

---

## Key Principles of Cost Management

1. **Visibility**: Understand where your money is going, across services, departments, and projects.
2. **Accountability**: Assign ownership for costs via tagging and budgeting.
3. **Optimization**: Reduce spend through automation, scaling, and reserved pricing.
4. **Governance**: Set policies to avoid waste and overprovisioning.
5. **Forecasting**: Plan ahead for seasonal or usage-driven variability.

---

## Azure Cost Management and Billing

Azure offers a suite of built-in tools for monitoring, analyzing, and optimizing spending.

**Tools:**

| Tool/Service | Purpose |
|---|---|
| **Cost Management + Billing** | Monitor usage, analyze spend, set budgets |
| **Azure Advisor** | Recommendations for cost, performance, availability, security |
| **Azure Monitor** | Track metrics and logs related to consumption |
| **Azure Pricing Calculator** | Estimate costs for new services or deployments |
| **Azure Reservations** | Prepay for long-term capacity to save on costs |

## Tracking Costs by Resource

Use Azure Cost Management to break down spend by:

- **Service** (e.g., Synapse, Data Factory)
- **Resource group**
- **Tags** (e.g., Project, Owner, Environment)
- **Subscription**

**Best Practice:** Apply cost analysis filters for monthly trends, daily spikes, and forecast estimates.

## Resource Tagging for Cost Attribution

Tags allow you to label resources with metadata such as:

- Project = RetailAnalytics

- Owner = frahaan.hussain
- Environment = Production
- Department = DataScience

**Tagging Example (CLI):**

az tag create—resource-id /subscriptions/abc/resourceGroups/rg/providers/Microsoft.Synapse/workspaces/myworkspace \

—tags Project=ChurnPrediction Environment=Prod

**Use Cases:**

- Allocate costs back to business units.
- Enable showback and chargeback models.
- Identify orphaned or unused resources.

---

## Cost Optimization Strategies by Service

**Azure Synapse Analytics**

- **Use serverless SQL for ad hoc queries** instead of dedicated pools.
- **Pause dedicated pools during idle hours.**
- **Use materialized views** for expensive aggregations to avoid recomputation.

- **Monitor DWU usage** with Synapse Studio and Azure Monitor.
- **Leverage reserved capacity** for predictable workloads.

**Azure Data Lake Storage Gen2**

- **Enable lifecycle management** to move infrequently accessed data to Cool or Archive tiers.
- **Compress data using Parquet or Avro** to reduce storage and read costs.
- **Avoid unnecessary data duplication** across zones (raw, curated, trusted).

```
{
"rules": [
{
"enabled": true,
"name": "MoveToCoolAfter30Days",
"type": "Lifecycle",
"definition": {
"actions": {
"baseBlob": {
"tierToCool": {
"daysAfterModificationGreaterThan": 30
```

```
}
}
},
"filters": {
"blobTypes": ["blockBlob"],
"prefixMatch": ["raw/"]
}
}
}
]
}
```

**Azure Data Factory**

- **Consolidate pipelines** to reduce overhead and activity count.
- **Use SSIS Integration Runtime only when necessary** due to higher cost.
- **Choose appropriate compute types** for Mapping Data Flows (Auto-Resolve for scale, MemoryOptimized for heavy joins).
- **Monitor pipeline run duration** to find inefficiencies.

### Azure SQL and Cosmos DB

- **Use auto-pausing and auto-scaling** for serverless SQL where possible.
- **Enable query performance insights** to identify costly or redundant queries.
- **Partition Cosmos DB** effectively to reduce RU consumption.

### Azure Machine Learning

- **Use low-priority VMs** for training experiments.
- **Shut down idle compute clusters** with idle timeout settings.
- **Track experiments by cost using tags.**
- **Use the estimator class** in the SDK to compare compute profiles before training.

---

## Budgeting and Alerts

Use **Budgets** in Azure Cost Management to:

- Set monthly/quarterly spending thresholds.
- Automatically notify owners when thresholds are breached.
- Trigger actions such as disabling services or sending alerts to Teams/Slack.

**Create a Budget Example (Portal):**

- Scope: Subscription or resource group
- Budget: £5,000/month
- Alert: At 80% (email to owner), 100% (disable non-prod resources via automation)

**CLI Example:**

az consumption budget create—amount 1000—time-grain Monthly \

—name dev-budget—category cost—start-date 2025-01-01 \

—end-date 2025-12-31—resource-group rg-dev

## Reserved Instances and Savings Plans

For long-term workloads, Azure offers:

- **Reserved Instances** for VMs and Synapse Dedicated Pools (save up to 72%).
- **Savings Plans** for compute across multiple services (more flexible).

**Best Practice:** Use Azure Advisor to identify eligible workloads for reservation.

## Automating Cost Control

**Use Logic Apps or Azure Automation to:**

- Auto-delete unused dev environments after hours.
- Scale down test clusters on weekends.
- Notify owners when spend crosses budget via webhook or email.
- Archive data older than X days from ADLS or SQL.

**Example Logic App:**

- Trigger: Daily at 6 PM
- Action: Query for VMs with tag Environment=Dev
- Condition: Uptime > 8 hours
- Action: Shutdown VM

---

## Reporting and Dashboards

Build custom dashboards using:

- **Azure Cost Management Reports**
- **Power BI with Cost Management connector**
- **Workbooks in Azure Monitor**
- **Excel export for reconciliation**

**Sample Power BI Metrics:**

- Monthly cost per workspace
- DWU usage per Synapse pool
- Number of pipeline runs vs compute time
- Storage tier usage across containers

---

## Governance Best Practices

- **Define cost accountability per team.**
- **Standardize tag taxonomy** (enforce with Azure Policy).
- **Review Azure Advisor monthly.**
- **Enable cost anomaly detection.**
- **Limit spend in dev/test with quotas or policy restrictions.**

---

## Summary

Effective cost control and resource management in Azure is not a one-time effort—it's an ongoing practice that spans strategy, tooling, automation, and culture. With the right governance model in place, organizations can gain full visibility into cloud spending, enforce accountability, optimize usage, and ensure long-term sustainability of their data platform investments.

Azure's comprehensive cost management capabilities, when paired with service-specific tuning and proactive monitoring, empower data teams to deliver innovation without compromising on financial efficiency. As we conclude the chapter, we've laid a secure, well-governed, and cost-efficient foundation for leveraging Azure data services to their fullest potential.

# Chapter 10: Future Trends and Innovations in Azure Data Services

## Evolving Cloud-Native Data Architectures

Cloud-native data architectures are transforming how organizations design, build, and scale analytics systems. With the explosive growth of data, a shift toward elasticity, modularity, and automation has become critical. Azure continues to evolve its platform to support this modern approach, integrating cutting-edge technologies, managed services, and architectural patterns that enable agility, performance, and innovation.

This section explores how cloud-native principles are reshaping data ecosystems. We'll examine core architectural shifts, Azure-native service innovations, emerging design patterns like data mesh and data fabric, and how to prepare for a future where agility, scale, and data-driven decision-making are the norm.

---

### What Is a Cloud-Native Data Architecture?

A cloud-native data architecture is designed to fully leverage the benefits of the cloud:

- **Elasticity**: Auto-scale resources based on demand.
- **Modularity**: Decoupled components that are independently deployable.
- **Resilience**: Fault-tolerant design to support high availability.

- **Observability**: Built-in logging, monitoring, and tracing.
- **Automation**: Infrastructure as code, CI/CD, and self-healing workflows.

Traditional monolithic data warehouses are giving way to architectures that are:

- API-driven
- Containerized
- Event-streamed
- Metadata-aware
- Federated and distributed

---

## Azure Services Powering Cloud-Native Architectures

Azure provides a robust foundation for building cloud-native data platforms:

| Azure Service | Cloud-Native Functionality |
|---|---|
| Azure Synapse Analytics | Unified analytics with serverless and dedicated engines |
| Azure Data Factory | Code-free, scalable data orchestration with triggers and monitoring |
| Azure Data Lake Gen2 | Massively scalable, tiered storage with hierarchical namespaces |
| Azure Kubernetes Service (AKS) | Microservices and container orchestration |
| Azure Event Hubs | Real-time event ingestion |
| Azure Stream Analytics | Real-time processing at scale |
| Azure Functions | Event-driven compute for lightweight, stateless tasks |
| Azure Cosmos DB | Globally distributed, multi-model database |

These services can be composed into modular architectures that handle data ingestion, transformation, storage, governance, and consumption with high flexibility and automation.

---

## Evolution of Data Platforms: From Monolith to Mesh

**Traditional Data Warehouse:**

- Centralized schema and compute
- Long ingestion-to-insight delays
- Poor fit for streaming, semi-structured data

**Modern Data Lakehouse:**

- Combines raw data lake storage with warehouse-like performance
- Supports batch and stream processing
- Ideal for ML and exploratory analytics

**Emerging Trend: Data Mesh**

- **Domain-oriented**: Each team owns and operates its data as a product.
- **Self-service platform**: Common tooling, governance, and infrastructure.
- **Federated governance**: Global policies, decentralized execution.
- Azure enables this via Synapse, Purview, and DevOps practices.

**Sample Mesh Design in Azure:**

- Each domain team has:
  - Its own Synapse workspace
  - Its own ADLS Gen2 container
  - Shared access to centralized Purview and CI/CD pipeline templates

---

## Event-Driven and Serverless Patterns

Cloud-native systems favor event-driven architectures that enable real-time responsiveness.

**Example Use Case: Retail Transaction Processing**

1. **Event Hub** captures point-of-sale data.
2. **Azure Function** cleans and enriches the data.
3. **Stream Analytics** computes hourly sales aggregates.
4. **Synapse** stores aggregated data for historical analysis.
5. **Power BI** delivers dashboards with real-time updates.

These components are loosely coupled and scale independently.

## Declarative Infrastructure and GitOps

Cloud-native architecture thrives on **Infrastructure as Code (IaC)**:

- **ARM** / **Bicep** for Azure resource templates
- **Terraform** for cloud-agnostic deployments
- **GitHub Actions** / **Azure DevOps** for CI/CD pipelines

**Benefits:**

- Versioned infrastructure
- Consistent environments (dev/test/prod)
- Automated rollback and promotion
- Auditable deployments

**Sample Bicep Snippet for Synapse Workspace:**

```
resource synapse 'Microsoft.Synapse/workspaces@2021-06-01' = {
name: 'analytics-dev'
location: 'eastus'
properties: {
defaultDataLakeStorage: {
accountUrl: 'https://datalake.dfs.core.windows.net'
filesystem: 'raw'
}
}
}
```

## Microservices and Data APIs

To decouple producers and consumers, data platforms increasingly expose **data-as-a-service** via APIs.

- Expose curated datasets via REST endpoints (Azure Functions, API Management)
- Apply authentication, throttling, and versioning
- Enable self-service consumption by internal and external consumers

Azure API Management can serve as a central gateway, while Cosmos DB or SQL Serverless pools back lightweight queries.

## Hybrid and Multi-Cloud Data Strategy

Organizations are rarely fully cloud-native overnight. Many require **hybrid** or **multi-cloud** support:

- Azure Arc enables management of resources across on-prem and other clouds.
- Azure Purview supports metadata ingestion from AWS, GCP, and SAP.
- Azure Synapse can query external data sources via PolyBase and linked services.

This allows organizations to evolve at their own pace without vendor lock-in.

---

## Principles of Modern Data Platform Design

1. **Design for Failure**

   ○ Implement retries, dead-letter queues, and failover.

2. **Automate Everything**

   ○ From provisioning to pipeline deployments.

3. **Observe and Optimize**

   ○ Use Azure Monitor and Application Insights for visibility.

4. **Secure by Default**

○ Private endpoints, managed identities, and policy enforcement.

5. **Data-as-a-Product**

○ Clear ownership, SLAs, documentation, and discoverability.

---

## Future-Ready Data Architectures

**Key characteristics:**

- **Composable**: Swap components without disrupting the system.
- **Metadata-driven**: Smart pipelines react to schema and quality metadata.
- **Policy-aware**: Auto-enforce governance at runtime (e.g., reject unclassified data).
- **Self-healing**: Detect and fix pipeline failures automatically.
- **AI-Augmented**: Auto-tune pipelines, recommend joins, summarize queries.

---

## Best Practices

- **Modularize pipelines** into reusable templates.
- **Use containerization** (Docker, AKS) for ML scoring services.

- **Adopt serverless** options for transient or spiky workloads.
- **Benchmark performance** with built-in telemetry before committing to scale.
- **Consolidate metadata** using Purview as a source of truth.

---

## Summary

Cloud-native data architectures represent the evolution of how modern enterprises manage, consume, and govern their data. Azure's robust service offerings, from Synapse to Data Factory to Purview, enable the construction of scalable, modular, and intelligent systems that adapt to change.

By embracing principles such as elasticity, automation, observability, and modularity, organizations can future-proof their data platforms—ensuring they're not only capable of handling today's demands but also ready for tomorrow's innovations. In the next section, we'll explore how artificial intelligence is becoming a core driver of these next-generation data platforms.

# The Role of AI in Data Platforms

Artificial Intelligence (AI) has become more than a technological trend—it is now a foundational layer in modern data platforms. AI transforms how data is collected, processed, analyzed, and acted upon. In Azure, AI-driven capabilities are deeply embedded across services such as Synapse Analytics, Azure Machine Learning, Azure Cognitive Services, and Azure Data Factory, enabling organizations to automate, predict, classify, and personalize experiences at scale.

This section explores the multifaceted role of AI in data platforms—from augmenting data pipelines with intelligent automation to enabling real-time decisioning and building AI-native analytics solutions. We will also review real-world use cases, architectural patterns, and best practices that illustrate how AI can unlock the next generation of data insights and business value.

## AI as a Native Layer in the Azure Ecosystem

In Azure, AI is not an add-on—it is integrated into the fabric of the data platform.

| Azure Service | AI Capability |
|---|---|
| **Azure Synapse Analytics** | T-SQL PREDICT() with ONNX models, integration with Azure ML |
| **Azure Data Factory** | Entity recognition, sentiment scoring, anomaly detection via Cognitive Services |
| **Azure Cognitive Services** | Pre-trained APIs for vision, speech, language, and decision-making |
| **Azure Machine Learning** | End-to-end model development and deployment |
| **Power BI** | AI visuals, smart narratives, and Q&A with natural language |
| **Azure OpenAI** | Generative AI for summarization, classification, search, and synthesis |

This integration allows organizations to infuse intelligence directly into pipelines, applications, dashboards, and workflows.

## Intelligent Data Processing Pipelines

AI enables smarter ETL/ELT processes by introducing capabilities such as:

- **Automated anomaly detection** in data flows
- **Entity recognition and PII redaction**
- **Sentiment analysis** for customer feedback
- **Image and video processing** for unstructured media data
- **Language translation** for global data pipelines

**Example: Cognitive Services in Data Factory**

Using the built-in ADF **Cognitive Services Linked Service**, you can enrich text data with sentiment scores:

1. Ingest customer reviews into a Data Lake.
2. Use a Data Flow that calls Text Analytics API to score sentiment.
3. Store results in a trusted layer for Power BI reporting.

```
{
"source": "reviews.csv",
"activity": "TextAnalytics",
"outputs": {
"SentimentScore": "textAnalytics().sentiment"
}
}
```

This enables real-time customer satisfaction monitoring without building a custom model.

---

## AI-Augmented Data Exploration and BI

AI empowers business users to explore data more intuitively:

- **Natural Language Queries**: Power BI Q&A allows users to type questions like "Total revenue by month" and get visual answers instantly.
- **Decomposition Tree**: Analyze key drivers automatically.
- **Smart Narratives**: Auto-generate textual summaries of visual insights.
- **Quick Insights**: AI detects correlations, outliers, and clusters in data.

These capabilities reduce the dependency on analysts for simple insights and democratize data understanding across the organization.

---

## Machine Learning for Predictive Analytics

ML models enable organizations to move beyond hindsight into foresight. Examples include:

- **Customer churn prediction**
- **Inventory demand forecasting**
- **Credit risk modeling**

- **Predictive maintenance for industrial assets**

**Workflow in Azure:**

1. **Data Prep**: Use Synapse or Data Factory to engineer features.
2. **Model Training**: Use Azure ML with AutoML or custom scripts.
3. **Model Deployment**: Expose as REST API or T-SQL model in Synapse.
4. **Scoring and Action**: Use pipelines or dashboards to act on predictions.

**Python Snippet Using AutoML:**

```
from azureml.train.automl import AutoMLConfig

automl_config = AutoMLConfig(

task='classification',

training_data=dataset,

label_column_name='Churn',

compute_target=compute_cluster,

iterations=20,

primary_metric='AUC_weighted'

)
```

This lowers the barrier to entry for predictive analytics and accelerates time to value.

## Real-Time AI in Event-Driven Architectures

AI is increasingly embedded in **real-time systems**, enabling immediate responses to events.

**Example: Fraud Detection Pipeline**

1. **Event Hub** ingests credit card transactions.
2. **Azure Stream Analytics** performs feature extraction.
3. **Azure ML Endpoint** scores each transaction for fraud probability.
4. **Azure Function** routes high-risk transactions for manual review.

This pattern combines streaming, ML scoring, and intelligent alerting—delivering AI-powered decisioning at millisecond latency.

## AI for Data Quality and Observability

AI can also enhance platform operations:

- **Anomaly detection** in data freshness, completeness, or schema drift.
- **Forecasting** for data load volumes and pipeline throughput.
- **Root cause analysis** for failed data jobs.

Azure Monitor and Log Analytics allow you to instrument telemetry and apply AI-based analytics to operational data.

## Generative AI and Language Models

The rise of large language models (LLMs), like those accessed via **Azure OpenAI**, introduces new possibilities:

- **Semantic search** across enterprise documents
- **Automated report generation** and insights summarization
- **Conversational agents** for internal data platforms
- **Code generation** and optimization of SQL and Spark scripts

**Example: Summarizing a Dataset**

```
from openai import AzureOpenAI

prompt = "Summarize key trends in this CSV data about website traffic."

response = AzureOpenAI.Completion.create(engine="text-davinci", prompt=prompt)

print(response.text)
```

Such capabilities allow organizations to process and understand unstructured data at scale.

---

## AI-Enhanced Data Governance

AI also plays a critical role in governance:

- **Classify data** automatically using ML models (e.g., identify PII, health records).

- **Detect sensitive data movement** across regions or boundaries.
- **Suggest glossary terms** or metadata using semantic tagging.

Azure Purview integrates AI for automatic classification and lineage inference—reducing manual workload for data stewards.

## Ethical AI and Responsible Deployment

With great power comes responsibility. Azure supports responsible AI practices through:

- **Fairness**: Tools for bias detection and mitigation.
- **Explainability**: SHAP and LIME integration for model transparency.
- **Accountability**: Logging, monitoring, and access control for all AI services.
- **Human oversight**: Review loops in high-risk decisions (e.g., loan approvals, diagnoses).

**Best Practice:** Use Azure's **Responsible AI Dashboard** to assess and validate models before deployment.

## Best Practices for Embedding AI

1. **Start with business outcomes** and choose models to match.
2. **Use prebuilt AI** (Cognitive Services) for common tasks before building from scratch.

3. **Integrate with existing pipelines** using ADF, Synapse, or APIs.
4. **Instrument everything** for visibility and continuous improvement.
5. **Use managed services** to reduce operational overhead.
6. **Train multidisciplinary teams**—combine domain, analytics, and ML expertise.

---

## Summary

AI is revolutionizing how data platforms operate, interact, and deliver value. From enriching raw data and augmenting pipelines to enabling real-time prediction and powering self-service analytics, the integration of AI within Azure creates intelligent systems that learn, adapt, and act.

As AI continues to evolve, it will become an inseparable part of every data strategy—not just as a technology, but as a mindset. Organizations that embrace AI holistically will gain the agility, insight, and automation necessary to lead in a data-driven world.

In the next section, we'll explore how emerging technologies like quantum computing could further redefine the boundaries of what's possible in data analytics.

# Quantum Computing and Data Analytics

Quantum computing represents one of the most revolutionary advancements in computing technology since the advent of the classical computer. It introduces new paradigms for solving problems that are either intractable or extremely slow to resolve with traditional methods. While still in its early stages, quantum computing is beginning to intersect with data analytics in ways that will eventually redefine how we store, process, and analyze data—especially at hyperscale levels.

Microsoft's Azure Quantum platform makes quantum computing accessible to developers, researchers, and enterprises by offering a flexible, open ecosystem for experimenting with quantum hardware, hybrid quantum-classical workflows, and simulation environments. This section explores how quantum computing is positioned to transform data analytics, outlines current capabilities in Azure Quantum, and explains the implications for the future of enterprise data platforms.

## The Fundamentals of Quantum Computing

Quantum computing leverages principles from quantum mechanics—particularly **superposition**, **entanglement**, and **interference**—to perform computations fundamentally differently than classical computers.

- **Superposition** allows quantum bits (qubits) to exist in multiple states simultaneously.
- **Entanglement** creates dependencies between qubits that allow simultaneous processing of related values.
- **Interference** ensures that desirable outcomes are amplified while errors cancel out.

The result is exponential speedup for specific classes of problems, particularly:

- Combinatorial optimization
- Quantum chemistry simulations

- Linear algebra problems (e.g., matrix inversion)
- Cryptographic analysis
- Machine learning and data clustering

---

## Limitations of Classical Analytics Platforms

Even the most powerful classical computers hit barriers in certain domains:

- **NP-hard problems** such as optimal route planning, job scheduling, or portfolio optimization are computationally intensive and scale poorly.
- **Large matrix computations** required for ML and financial modeling become time- and memory-intensive.
- **Factorization-based cryptography** faces theoretical risks from quantum attacks.
- **Monte Carlo simulations** require millions of iterations to converge to accurate results.

Quantum computing promises improvements in these areas by processing large solution spaces in parallel via superposition.

---

## Azure Quantum Overview

Azure Quantum is Microsoft's fully managed quantum cloud platform. It brings together:

- **Quantum hardware providers** (e.g., IonQ, Quantinuum, Rigetti, QCI)

- **Optimization solvers** (e.g., Microsoft's QIO and Toshiba's SBM)
- **Quantum development tools** (Q# language, QDK, Jupyter Notebooks)
- **Integration with Azure services** (storage, compute, ML, identity)

Developers can build hybrid workflows that mix quantum and classical components in a familiar cloud-native environment.

## Quantum-Inspired Optimization (QIO)

Most immediate impact today comes not from quantum computers, but **quantum-inspired optimization algorithms**. These algorithms simulate quantum mechanics principles on classical hardware and solve large-scale optimization problems efficiently.

### Example Use Case: Supply Chain Optimization

Azure Quantum can be used to solve a vehicle routing problem with constraints (fuel limits, delivery windows, load capacity) in seconds, which might take hours with traditional solvers.

**Python QIO Snippet:**

```
from azure.quantum.optimization import Problem, Term

terms = [

Term(w=1, indices=[0]),

Term(w=-1, indices=[1]),

Term(w=2, indices=[0, 1])
```

```
]

problem = Problem(name="simple-qio", terms=terms)

result = workspace.submit(problem)

print(result)
```

This technique is highly applicable in logistics, manufacturing, healthcare scheduling, and energy grid optimization.

## Quantum Algorithms for Data Analytics

Quantum algorithms are being explored and implemented for various data-related tasks:

| Task | Quantum Approach |
|---|---|
| **Clustering** | Quantum k-means, QAOA |
| **Dimensionality Reduction** | Quantum PCA |
| **Recommendation Engines** | Quantum Boltzmann Machines |
| **Anomaly Detection** | Quantum-enhanced autoencoders |
| **Portfolio Optimization** | QUBO formulations with QIO or QAOA |
| **Search & Sorting** | Grover's algorithm |

While these are largely experimental, they provide early signals of future capabilities where vast datasets can be processed in seconds through quantum acceleration.

## Hybrid Quantum-Classical Workflows

Azure Quantum supports hybrid workflows where quantum subroutines are embedded within classical pipelines.

**Architecture Example:**

1. **Ingest data** with Azure Data Factory or Event Hubs.
2. **Pre-process** using Azure Synapse or Azure ML.
3. **Invoke quantum solver** via Azure Quantum (QIO or hardware backend).
4. **Post-process and visualize** with Power BI or a custom app.

This allows existing applications to benefit from quantum improvements without full rewrites.

---

## Security and Quantum-Resistant Cryptography

As quantum computers mature, they will challenge traditional encryption methods like RSA and ECC. Azure is actively working on **post-quantum cryptography (PQC)** initiatives:

- Transitioning to **quantum-safe algorithms** (e.g., lattice-based cryptography).

- Ensuring secure communications for quantum-powered services.

- Preparing developers through **quantum threat modeling** and readiness guides.

Governments and banks are already piloting PQC in anticipation of the quantum era.

---

## Simulation and Emulation

For developers and researchers without access to quantum hardware, Azure provides emulators:

- **Quantum simulators** for debugging and experimentation.

- **Resource estimation tools** to understand qubit requirements.

- **Noise models** to simulate hardware imperfections.

This enables experimentation without costly infrastructure and prepares teams for future migration to real quantum devices.

---

## Real-World Applications Emerging Today

### Healthcare

- Optimize clinical trial matching

- Simulate molecular interactions

- Forecast ICU resource usage

### Finance

- Risk modeling across millions of scenarios

- Detect fraud patterns in sparse datasets

- Solve portfolio rebalancing problems

### Energy

- Balance renewable energy loads across grids

- Optimize pipeline routing and maintenance

- Forecast demand with stochastic variables

**Aerospace**

- Trajectory optimization for low-earth orbit
- Maintenance scheduling for fleets
- Quantum-enhanced fault prediction

These use cases, while still in early stages, show immense promise in scaling insights and decision-making far beyond current limits.

## Challenges and Considerations

Despite the promise, quantum computing remains an emerging field:

- **Limited qubit counts** and error rates restrict problem sizes.
- **Specialized skills** in quantum algorithms are rare.
- **Tooling maturity** still lags behind classical ML or cloud data engineering.
- **Cost**: Access to quantum hardware is often metered and expensive.

To mitigate these, Azure focuses on **democratizing access, offering training**, and **building abstraction layers** so data engineers and scientists can participate without deep quantum expertise.

## Preparing for the Quantum Future

Organizations can take steps today to prepare:

1. **Educate** teams on quantum principles and Azure Quantum tooling.
2. **Identify high-value optimization problems** that may benefit from quantum speedup.
3. **Partner with Microsoft or academic institutions** for pilot projects.
4. **Monitor quantum roadmap** from providers like IonQ, Quantinuum, and QCI.
5. **Start building hybrid pipelines** that can eventually offload to quantum accelerators.

---

## Summary

Quantum computing holds the potential to reshape the data analytics landscape—offering new ways to process, simulate, and optimize at speeds previously unimaginable. Azure Quantum stands at the forefront of this shift, enabling enterprises to explore quantum innovation while staying grounded in today's cloud-native workflows.

While still nascent, the implications are clear: data platforms of the future will not only be scalable and intelligent—they will also be quantum-aware. As with AI before it, early adopters of quantum technologies will gain a strategic edge in solving the world's hardest problems. In the final section of this chapter, we'll look at how to prepare your organization for continuous innovation in this ever-evolving ecosystem.

# Preparing for Continuous Innovation

In today's rapidly evolving digital landscape, the only constant is change. Data platforms, analytics tools, governance frameworks, and AI capabilities are advancing at an unprecedented pace. As we've seen throughout this chapter—from cloud-native architecture to quantum computing—staying ahead requires more than just technical upgrades. It demands a proactive, organizational commitment to **continuous innovation.**

This section provides a roadmap for preparing your organization to adapt, evolve, and thrive in the face of constant technological change. We'll explore the cultural, architectural, and operational shifts required to build a sustainable innovation engine powered by Azure's ecosystem. Whether you're modernizing legacy systems or leading greenfield projects, these practices will help you future-proof your data platform and workforce.

---

## Why Continuous Innovation Matters

Continuous innovation is essential for:

- **Staying competitive** in fast-moving industries.
- **Unlocking new business models** through data products and AI.
- **Improving agility** to respond to market shifts and disruptions.
- **Retaining top talent** by offering modern, engaging tools and processes.
- **Driving measurable ROI** from cloud investments.

In a data context, innovation means being able to rapidly ingest new data types, adopt emerging tools, build smarter analytics, and scale without friction.

---

## Principles of a Continuously Innovative Data Organization

1. **Agility over Perfection**: Prioritize incremental delivery over long-term "big bang" projects.
2. **Platform Thinking**: Build reusable, modular data and AI services that support multiple use cases.
3. **DevOps and MLOps First**: Treat infrastructure, pipelines, and models as code.
4. **Product Mindset**: Treat data assets as products with roadmaps, ownership, SLAs, and feedback loops.
5. **Learning Culture**: Continuously train teams on emerging tech and methodologies.
6. **Feedback-Driven Development**: Build tight loops between users, analysts, engineers, and decision-makers.

---

## Evolving Architecture for Change

Designing systems for adaptability is key to sustaining innovation.

### Adopt Modular, Decoupled Components

Use microservices or service-oriented design with clear contracts (e.g., APIs, schema registries).

- Swap or upgrade components independently.
- Reduce downstream ripple effects of change.

- Enable A/B testing and experimentation.

**Example:**

- **Data Ingestion**: Event Hubs
- **Transformation**: Azure Data Factory or Spark
- **Storage**: ADLS Gen2 (bronze/silver/gold)
- **Serving Layer**: Power BI / Synapse / APIs

Each layer can evolve independently as new tools or requirements arise.

---

## Implement DevOps and MLOps

Treat infrastructure, pipelines, and models as versioned, testable, and deployable artifacts.

- **Use GitHub Actions or Azure DevOps** to automate deployment of Synapse workspaces, Data Factory pipelines, ML models.
- **Use Terraform or Bicep** for infrastructure provisioning.
- **Use MLflow or Azure ML Pipelines** to track and manage model experiments.

**CI/CD for Synapse Workspace (Bicep + DevOps):**

trigger:

branches:

```
include:
- main
jobs:
- job: DeploySynapse
pool:
vmImage: ubuntu-latest
steps:
- task: AzureCLI@2
inputs:
azureSubscription: 'AzureDevOpsServiceConnection'
scriptType: 'bash'
scriptLocation: 'inlineScript'
inlineScript: |
az deployment group create—resource-group rg-data \
—template-file synapse.bicep \
—parameters environment=dev
```

This allows frequent, risk-reduced innovation through smaller, reversible changes.

---

## Establish a Data Product Framework

Instead of building projects, build products. Treat datasets, APIs, dashboards, and ML models as **long-lived digital assets**.

| Aspect | Traditional Project | Data Product |
|---|---|---|
| Ownership | Temporary | Persistent with named owner |
| Lifecycle | Build-Deliver | Continuous improvement and support |
| Success Metric | On-time delivery | User adoption, value delivered |
| Documentation | Optional | Required, discoverable in catalog |
| SLAs | Rare | Enforced for uptime, quality, freshness |

**Example:** A customer segmentation model is a product—used by marketing, sales, and customer service. It has a roadmap (new features, re-train frequency), documentation, APIs, and monitoring.

## Drive Culture Change

Tools and architecture matter—but culture is the engine of innovation. Foster a mindset that encourages experimentation, learning, and collaboration.

**Initiatives to Promote Culture Shift:**

- **Innovation Sprints**: Cross-functional time-boxed experiments with a defined scope.
- **Fail-Fast Labs**: Safe environments to try bleeding-edge features (e.g., Azure OpenAI, Synapse Link).
- **Tech Talks and Internal Hackathons**: Share knowledge and build community.
- **Cloud Champions Program**: Nominate leaders to evangelize best practices.

Leadership support is critical. Innovation must be incentivized, recognized, and aligned with business goals.

---

## Invest in Data Literacy and Skills

Innovation requires empowered people. Focus on developing skill sets across roles:

- **Business Users**: Self-service BI, data storytelling, Power BI
- **Data Engineers**: Cloud-native pipelines, Spark, streaming
- **Data Scientists**: ML engineering, responsible AI
- **Analysts**: DAX, SQL, AI-assisted analytics (e.g., Copilot in Power BI)
- **Architects**: Governance, performance tuning, FinOps

Use tools like Microsoft Learn, LinkedIn Learning, internal bootcamps, and certifications (e.g., DP-203, AI-102).

---

## Enable Experimentation

Set up sandboxes and test environments that allow innovation without risk:

- **Use separate subscriptions or resource groups** for development.
- **Apply Azure Policies and budgets** to prevent overuse.
- **Tag and track** experiments for visibility and learning.

This helps teams test new services, evaluate new SDKs, and prototype ideas quickly.

## Measure Innovation Outcomes

Track metrics that go beyond velocity or cost:

- **Time to value**: How quickly can new ideas reach production?
- **Adoption rate**: Are new tools, features, or data products being used?
- **Data coverage**: How many domains are actively governed and modeled?
- **Team satisfaction**: Are people empowered, engaged, and proud of their work?

Use dashboards in Power BI to make innovation visible and celebrated.

## Leverage Azure for Continuous Improvement

Azure's platform is designed for evolution:

- **Preview features** in services like Synapse and Data Factory.
- **Feature flags** and AB testing in App Services or API Management.
- **Usage telemetry** in Application Insights and Azure Monitor.

- **Innovation insights** via Azure Advisor and Cost Management.

Let telemetry guide your roadmap. Let usage inform what to iterate next.

---

## Best Practices

1. **Automate everything**—from infrastructure to deployment to testing.
2. **Use version control** for data models, pipelines, notebooks, and dashboards.
3. **Promote ownership** of data products and platform components.
4. **Create innovation playbooks** to guide experimentation.
5. **Build innovation KPIs** into your OKRs and strategic goals.
6. **Balance stability with agility**—use ring deployments or blue/green environments.

---

## Summary

Innovation is no longer a phase—it's a continuous loop of learning, adapting, and improving. In the Azure ecosystem, organizations have all the tools and services needed to build resilient, adaptive, and intelligent data platforms. But true transformation comes from people, processes, and mindset.

By embracing platform thinking, fostering a culture of experimentation, investing in skills, and operationalizing DevOps and product models, enterprises can unlock a future of perpetual innovation. The most successful data organizations of tomorrow will not just manage change—they will lead it.

As we move into the final chapter of this book, we'll provide a comprehensive set of appendices, references, and additional resources to help you continue this journey.

# Chapter 11: Appendices

## Glossary of Terms

This glossary provides clear definitions of key terms, acronyms, and concepts used throughout the book. Whether you're a newcomer to Azure or an experienced practitioner, this reference section is designed to reinforce your understanding and provide clarity as you navigate Azure's diverse and rapidly evolving data ecosystem.

### A

**Access Control List (ACL)**

A list of permissions attached to an object (such as a file or directory) that defines which users or system processes can access that object and what operations they can perform.

**Active Directory (AD)**

A directory service by Microsoft for Windows domain networks. Azure Active Directory (Azure AD) is the cloud-based version used for identity and access management in Azure environments.

**AI (Artificial Intelligence)**

A branch of computer science focused on building systems that can simulate intelligent behavior such as learning, reasoning, and self-correction.

**Analytics**

The process of discovering, interpreting, and communicating meaningful patterns in data. In Azure, analytics is enabled via tools like Synapse Analytics, Power BI, and Stream Analytics.

## B

### Blob Storage

Azure's object storage solution for the cloud, optimized for storing massive amounts of unstructured data including images, videos, documents, and backups.

### Bicep

A domain-specific language (DSL) for deploying Azure resources declaratively. It's a more concise and easier-to-read alternative to ARM templates.

### Big Data

Data that is high in volume, velocity, and variety, requiring advanced technologies and architectures to process and analyze effectively.

## C

### CI/CD (Continuous Integration/Continuous Deployment)

A DevOps practice that automates the integration and deployment of code changes, improving software delivery speed and quality.

### Cognitive Services

A suite of prebuilt AI services by Microsoft that provide APIs for tasks like language understanding, computer vision, speech recognition, and decision-making.

### Cosmos DB

Azure's globally distributed, multi-model database service that offers low latency and high availability with support for SQL, MongoDB, Cassandra, and other APIs.

**Cost Management**

Azure's toolset for tracking, analyzing, and optimizing spending across cloud resources.

---

## D

**Data Factory (ADF)**

A cloud-based data integration service that enables the creation of data-driven workflows for orchestrating and automating data movement and transformation.

**Data Lake**

A centralized repository that allows you to store structured and unstructured data at any scale. Azure Data Lake Storage Gen2 combines capabilities of hierarchical file systems with the scalability of object storage.

**Data Mesh**

A decentralized data architecture that treats data as a product and assigns ownership to cross-functional teams, enabling scalable, domain-oriented data practices.

**Data Pipeline**

A set of processes that move data from one system to another, potentially transforming it along the way. Built using ADF, Synapse Pipelines, or Databricks in Azure.

---

## E

**ETL/ELT (Extract, Transform, Load / Extract, Load, Transform)**

Data processing methods. ETL transforms data before loading it into a storage system, while ELT loads raw data first and transforms it later, often using the power of cloud data warehouses.

**Event Hub**

Azure's big data streaming platform and event ingestion service capable of receiving and processing millions of events per second.

**Exploratory Data Analysis (EDA)**

A method for analyzing data sets by summarizing their main characteristics, often using visual methods.

---

## F

**Feature Engineering**

The process of using domain knowledge to extract features from raw data that improve the performance of machine learning algorithms.

**Function App (Azure Functions)**

A serverless compute service that allows you to run event-triggered code without explicitly provisioning or managing infrastructure.

---

## G

**Governance**

Policies, roles, responsibilities, and processes that control how an organization's data and infrastructure are managed, protected, and audited.

**GitOps**

A modern approach to infrastructure automation using Git as a single source of truth and CI/CD pipelines to manage changes to infrastructure.

---

## H

### Hybrid Cloud

An IT architecture that incorporates some degree of workload portability, orchestration, and management across two or more environments, including public cloud and private data centers.

### Hierarchical Namespace

A file system structure in Azure Data Lake Gen2 that allows directories and files to be managed and accessed like a traditional file system.

---

## I

### IaC (Infrastructure as Code)

The management of infrastructure (networks, virtual machines, load balancers, etc.) in a descriptive model using code rather than manual processes.

### Identity and Access Management (IAM)

The framework of policies and technologies to ensure that the right individuals access the right resources at the right times for the right reasons.

---

## J

### JSON (JavaScript Object Notation)

A lightweight data-interchange format that is easy for humans to read and write, and for machines to parse and generate. Common in API responses and configuration files.

---

## K

### Kusto Query Language (KQL)

A read-only request language used to process data and return results in Azure Monitor, Log Analytics, and Azure Data Explorer.

### Kubernetes (AKS)

An open-source container orchestration system for automating software deployment, scaling, and management. Azure Kubernetes Service (AKS) offers a managed version.

---

## L

### Lineage

The data's origin, what happens to it, and where it moves over time. Important for traceability, auditing, and debugging data issues.

### Log Analytics

A feature of Azure Monitor that collects and analyzes log data from various resources, enabling deep insights and custom queries.

---

## M

### Managed Identity

An Azure feature that provides automatically managed identities for Azure services to use when connecting to other resources securely.

### Metadata

Descriptive information about data, such as its source, type, owner, and usage policies.

**MLOps**

A set of practices that unify ML system development (Dev) and ML system operations (Ops) to streamline deployment, monitoring, and governance of ML models.

---

## N

**Notebook**

An interactive development environment that supports live code, equations, visualizations, and explanatory text—commonly used in Synapse and Azure ML Studio.

---

## O

**OpenAI Service (Azure)**

A managed service providing access to OpenAI's models (GPT, Codex, DALL·E) via REST APIs, enabling language generation, code completion, and more.

**Observability**

The ability to understand the internal state of a system through logs, metrics, and traces—critical for debugging and performance optimization.

---

## P

**Parquet**

A columnar storage format that is optimized for read-heavy analytic workloads. Commonly used in big data processing.

**Purview**

Azure's data governance and cataloging platform, offering metadata scanning, classification, data lineage, and search capabilities.

**Power BI**

Microsoft's business analytics tool that provides interactive visualizations and business intelligence capabilities with a simple interface.

---

## Q

**Q#**

A quantum programming language used with Microsoft's Quantum Development Kit (QDK) for developing quantum algorithms.

---

## R

**Role-Based Access Control (RBAC)**

A method of regulating access to resources based on the roles of individual users within an organization.

**Resource Group**

A container that holds related Azure resources. Allows for easier management, monitoring, and access control.

---

## S

**Serverless**

A cloud computing model where the cloud provider manages the server infrastructure. You just write and deploy code, and it's executed on demand.

**Synapse Analytics**

An integrated analytics service in Azure that brings together big data and data warehousing.

---

## T

**Terraform**

An open-source IaC software tool that provides a consistent CLI workflow to manage hundreds of cloud services.

**T-SQL**

Transact-SQL, Microsoft's extension to SQL, used primarily with SQL Server and Azure SQL Database.

---

## U

**Unified Data Platform**

A system that combines multiple data storage, processing, and analysis tools under one architecture for streamlined data operations.

---

## V

**Virtual Network (VNet)**

Azure's network service that enables securely isolated networks and secure communication between Azure resources.

---

## W

### Workspace (Azure ML / Synapse)

A centralized environment for managing related services, assets, and resources used in machine learning or analytics workflows.

## X

### XML (eXtensible Markup Language)

A markup language that defines rules for encoding documents in a format that is both human-readable and machine-readable.

## Y

### YAML (YAML Ain't Markup Language)

A human-readable data serialization standard often used for configuration files in DevOps and cloud environments.

## Z

### Zone Redundancy

The distribution of resources across different availability zones to ensure high availability and resilience in case of datacenter failures.

This glossary serves as a foundational reference as you continue to explore and build with Azure data services. In the next section, we'll share a curated list of resources for expanding your knowledge and staying current with the latest developments in Azure's data ecosystem.

# Resources for Further Learning

The journey of mastering Azure data services and architectures is a continuous one. As the platform rapidly evolves, staying up-to-date with the latest capabilities, patterns, and best practices is essential for professionals across all levels—from data engineers and architects to business analysts and decision-makers.

This section provides a comprehensive collection of learning resources categorized by format and focus area. These resources include official Microsoft documentation, community-led platforms, structured certifications, technical blogs, video series, sandbox environments, and ongoing development opportunities to keep your skills sharp and relevant in the ever-changing cloud landscape.

## Official Microsoft Resources

### Microsoft Learn

Microsoft Learn (https://learn.microsoft.com[1]) is the central hub for interactive, hands-on, self-paced learning content. It's ideal for structured paths and provides free learning modules that cover everything from beginner fundamentals to advanced architectural guidance.

**Recommended Learning Paths:**

- Azure Fundamentals (AZ-900)
- Azure Data Fundamentals (DP-900)
- Azure Data Engineer Associate (DP-203)

1. https://learn.microsoft.com/

- Azure AI Fundamentals (AI-900)
- Designing and Implementing an Azure Data Solution (DP-420)

**Features:**

- Interactive coding environments (sandbox)
- Knowledge checks
- Role-based learning paths
- Integration with Microsoft certifications

**Microsoft Documentation**

Each Azure service has detailed, live documentation updated regularly:

- https://learn.microsoft.com/en-us/azure/synapse-analytics/
- https://learn.microsoft.com/en-us/azure/data-factory/
- https://learn.microsoft.com/en-us/azure/data-lake-store/
- https://learn.microsoft.com/en-us/azure/machine-learning/
- https://learn.microsoft.com/en-us/azure/purview/

Documentation includes quickstarts, how-to guides, API references, and architecture blueprints.

---

## Certification and Exam Preparation

Azure certifications are industry-recognized credentials that validate your cloud skills.

**Key Certifications:**

- **DP-203**: Data Engineering on Microsoft Azure

  Focuses on data ingestion, transformation, storage, security, and performance optimization using Synapse, Data Lake, ADF, and more.

- **DP-900**: Azure Data Fundamentals

  A foundational exam covering core concepts in relational, non-relational, big data, and analytics on Azure.

- **AI-900**: Azure AI Fundamentals

  Covers AI workloads, ML basics, and responsible AI principles using Azure AI services.

**Preparation Resources:**

- Microsoft Learn Exam Paths
- Whizlabs, A Cloud Guru, and Pluralsight practice tests
- GitHub repositories with sample notebooks and scenarios

- Exam-specific YouTube series by Microsoft MVPs

---

## Hands-On Labs and Sandboxes

Learning by doing is the most effective way to retain cloud skills. The following environments offer safe, free, or low-cost hands-on experience.

**Microsoft Learn Sandbox**

Many modules include free access to Azure resources without requiring a personal subscription.

**Azure Free Account**

- 12-month free tier and $200 credit
- https://azure.microsoft.com/free/

**GitHub Repos for Labs**

- **Azure Data Fundamentals GitHub Repo**: Real-world examples aligned with DP-900
- **Synapse Analytics End-to-End Demo**:https://github.com/Azure/SynapseNotebooks
- **Azure OpenAI Samples**:https://github.com/Azure/openai-samples

---

## Community and Forums

Engaging with the community can help you troubleshoot issues faster, discover tips and tricks, and stay current with best practices.

### Microsoft Tech Community

- https://techcommunity.microsoft.com[2]
- Sections for every Azure service with blogs, discussions, and events

### Stack Overflow

- Use tags like azure-data-factory, azure-synapse, azure-data-lake, azure-ml for targeted Q&A.

### GitHub Discussions

- Many official Azure samples and SDKs host community-driven discussions.

### Reddit Communities

- r/AZURE, r/DataEngineering, and r/MachineLearning

### Meetup and Local User Groups

Look for Azure-focused meetups or user groups in your area. Microsoft Reactor hosts regular virtual and in-person events featuring speakers from the field.

2. https://techcommunity.microsoft.com/

## Blogs and Technical Content

These curated blogs offer valuable insights into real-world implementations, product updates, and advanced topics.

### Microsoft Tech Blogs

- https://techcommunity.microsoft.com/t5/azure-architecture-blog
- https://techcommunity.microsoft.com/t5/azure-synapse-analytics/bg-p/AzureSynapseAnalytics

### Notable Independent Blogs:

- SQLBI.com (Power BI, DAX, Synapse)
- Advancing Analytics (Synapse, Fabric, ML)
- Data Platform MVP blogs (search viahttps://mvp.microsoft.com[3])

### Newsletters:

- Azure Weekly (https://azureweekly.info[4])
- Data Elixir (https://dataelixir.com[5])
- The Morning Paper (academic research in simple language)

---

3. https://mvp.microsoft.com/
4. https://azureweekly.info/
5. https://dataelixir.com/

## Videos and Channels

Video learning can be a helpful supplement to written content and ideal for walkthroughs, demos, and conceptual deep dives.

**Microsoft Azure YouTube Channel**

- https://www.youtube.com/user/windowsazure
- Weekly updates, Ignite sessions, and service intros

**Microsoft Mechanics**

- Deep dive into Azure technologies and architecture
- https://www.youtube.com/c/MicrosoftMechanics

**Pluralsight and LinkedIn Learning**

Paid platforms with structured courses. Look for authors like Tim Warner, Lynn Langit, and Alan Smith.

**Azure Friday**

- Weekly short videos hosted by Scott Hanselman
- Interviews with Microsoft engineers and product leads
- https://azure.microsoft.com/en-us/resources/videos/azure-friday/

---

## Emerging Technologies

Stay on top of what's next by following the evolution of quantum computing, AI, data mesh, and edge analytics.

**Azure Quantum**

- https://learn.microsoft.com/en-us/azure/quantum/

**Microsoft Fabric (Preview)**

- https://learn.microsoft.com/en-us/fabric/
- A unified SaaS platform that integrates Power BI, Synapse, and Data Factory

**Azure AI and OpenAI**

- https://learn.microsoft.com/en-us/azure/cognitive-services/
- https://learn.microsoft.com/en-us/azure/ai-services/openai/

---

## Academic and Research Resources

- Microsoft Research:https://www.microsoft.com/en-us/research/
- ArXiv.org for quantum, ML, and data pipeline innovation
- MIT OpenCourseWare: Intro to ML and Data Science

- HarvardX / EdX courses sponsored by Microsoft

---

## Staying Current

- **Follow Azure blogs**:https://azure.microsoft.com/en-us/blog/
- **Use RSS readers** to subscribe to your favorite documentation pages
- **Engage with Microsoft MVPs** on Twitter/X, LinkedIn, and YouTube
- **Attend Microsoft Ignite, Build, and Data Platform Summit** for roadmap insights

---

## Summary

There has never been a better time to learn and grow within the Azure data ecosystem. With a wide array of tools, communities, and educational resources available, practitioners at all stages of their careers can build expertise, stay relevant, and contribute meaningfully to modern, data-driven organizations.

Whether you're seeking certifications, building proof-of-concepts, deploying production systems, or exploring bleeding-edge innovations like generative AI and quantum computing, continuous learning will be your most valuable asset. Let this resource list be your compass as you navigate the exciting world of Azure data services.

## Sample Projects and Code Snippets

To truly master Azure's data ecosystem, it is essential to move beyond theory and into hands-on project work. This section provides a range of practical sample projects and code snippets that demonstrate real-world scenarios. Each project covers different Azure services, architectures, and use cases—from batch ingestion pipelines to AI-powered analytics and secure data governance setups. These samples are designed to be modular and reproducible, providing a foundation for customization, experimentation, and production deployment.

---

### Project 1: End-to-End Data Lakehouse with Synapse, Data Lake, and Power BI

**Objective:** Create a complete modern data lakehouse solution using Azure Synapse Analytics and Azure Data Lake Gen2, with Power BI as the reporting layer.

**Components Used:**

- Azure Data Lake Storage Gen2
- Azure Synapse Analytics (Serverless and Dedicated Pools)
- Azure Data Factory
- Azure Key Vault (for secure credentials)
- Power BI

**Steps:**

1. **Ingest Data Using Data Factory:**
   - Source: Sample CSVs in a public GitHub repo
   - Destination: Raw zone in ADLS Gen2

```
{
"type": "Copy",
"inputs": ["SourceBlobDataset"],
"outputs": ["RawADLSDataset"],
"translator": {
"type": "TabularTranslator",
"columnMappings": {
"CustomerName": "CustomerName",
"PurchaseAmount": "Amount"
}
}
}
```

2.

3. **Transform Data Using Synapse Pipelines:**
   - Clean and normalize data using SQL scripts and Spark notebooks.

- Save curated output in Parquet format to the trusted zone.

```
SELECT
CustomerName,
TRY_CAST(PurchaseAmount AS FLOAT) AS Amount,
GETDATE() AS LoadTimestamp
INTO trusted.Purchases
FROM raw.Purchases
```

4.

5. **Load into Synapse Dedicated Pool:**
   - Create external tables in Serverless
   - Load into performance-optimized tables for analytics
6. **Create Power BI Report:**
   - Connect to Synapse via DirectQuery
   - Build a dashboard showing purchase trends, top customers, anomalies

---

## Project 2: Real-Time Data Ingestion and Processing with Event Hubs and Stream Analytics

**Objective:** Build a real-time ingestion pipeline to process streaming IoT sensor data.

**Components:**

- Azure Event Hubs
- Azure Stream Analytics
- Azure SQL Database
- Azure Monitor (for diagnostics)

**Architecture:**

1. Simulated IoT devices send telemetry to Event Hubs.
2. Stream Analytics job processes and aggregates events.
3. Results are written to a SQL Database in near real time.

**Code Snippet: Stream Analytics Query**

```
SELECT
deviceId,
AVG(temperature) AS avgTemp,
System.Timestamp AS windowEnd
INTO
sqlOutput
FROM
eventHubInput
GROUP BY
```

TumblingWindow(minute, 5),

deviceId

---

## Project 3: Secure Data Platform with Role-Based Access Control and Purview

**Objective:** Build a secure, governed data platform with lineage, classification, and access control.

**Components:**

- Azure Data Lake Gen2
- Azure Purview
- Azure RBAC and ACLs
- Azure Active Directory Groups

**Key Actions:**

**Configure RBAC and ACLs on ADLS:**

az storage fs access set \

—path /finance \

—acl "user:12345678-1234-1234-1234-1234567890ab:rwx" \

—account-name mystorageaccount \

—file-system data

1.

2. **Scan Data Lake in Purview:**
   - Automatically classify fields (PII, Financial)
   - Assign glossary terms and ownership
3. **Use Lineage View to Trace Data Movement:**
   - From raw ingestion to BI reports
   - Validate governance policy compliance
4. **Integrate with Azure AD for fine-grained access:**
   - Developers: Read/Write to raw/curated
   - Analysts: Read-only to curated/trusted

---

## Project 4: Machine Learning with Synapse and Azure ML

**Objective:** Build a predictive model to forecast customer churn and integrate scoring into Synapse.

**Components:**

- Azure Synapse Analytics
- Azure Machine Learning Workspace
- Synapse Spark Pools
- Azure ML SDK (Python)

**Workflow:**

**Data Preparation in Synapse:**

```
SELECT
customer_id,
last_login_date,
purchase_frequency,
churned
INTO curated.customer_churn_data
FROM raw.customer_logs
```

1.

**Train Model with Azure ML AutoML:**

```
from azureml.train.automl import AutoMLConfig
automl_config = AutoMLConfig(
task='classification',
training_data=dataset,
label_column_name='churned',
compute_target=compute_cluster,
primary_metric='AUC_weighted'
)
```

2.

**Deploy Model as REST Endpoint:**

from azureml.core.webservice import AciWebservice

service = Model.deploy(workspace, "churn-model", models=[model], inference_config=inference_config, deployment_config=AciWebservice.deploy_configuration())

service.wait_for_deployment(show_output=True)

3.

4. **Invoke Model in Synapse Using Predict Function:**

- Register the model in Synapse with ONNX format
- Use PREDICT() in T-SQL to score incoming data

---

## Project 5: Metadata-Driven Pipeline Framework

**Objective:** Create a reusable metadata-driven ETL framework to reduce manual configuration.

**Components:**

- Azure Data Factory
- Azure SQL for metadata storage
- Parameterized pipelines
- Lookup activities and ForEach control flow

**SQL Metadata Table:**

```
CREATE TABLE PipelineMetadata (
SourceTableName VARCHAR(100),
TargetTableName VARCHAR(100),
CopyBehavior VARCHAR(20),
IsActive BIT
);
```

**ADF Control Pipeline Logic:**

1. Lookup active sources from metadata table.
2. Loop through each row using ForEach.
3. Use expressions to set dynamic source/target datasets.

**Expression Example:**

```
"@concat('CopyFrom', item().SourceTableName)"
```

## Code Repository Standards

All projects should follow best practices:

- Structure repos with /infra, /pipelines, /notebooks, /scripts, /docs
- Include README.md with setup steps, diagram, and use case description
- Use .env or Key Vault integration for secrets

- Implement error handling and logging (Log Analytics)

---

## Summary

These sample projects and code snippets offer practical guidance to start or refine your Azure data platform journey. They not only demonstrate technical capabilities but also reflect best practices in modular design, automation, and governance.

Each project is scalable and can be adapted to meet your organization's unique needs. Whether you're building prototypes or preparing for production rollouts, use these as a launching pad for innovation, collaboration, and mastery of Azure's powerful data ecosystem.

# API Reference Guide

Application Programming Interfaces (APIs) are a fundamental part of modern cloud data platforms. They provide programmatic access to services, enable automation of processes, and allow seamless integration across tools, environments, and applications. In Azure, nearly every service discussed in this book—such as Synapse Analytics, Data Factory, Data Lake, Purview, and Machine Learning—exposes rich APIs (often RESTful) to perform management, data, and operational tasks.

This section provides a comprehensive reference guide to commonly used APIs across Azure's data services. It includes endpoint structures, authentication methods, examples of real-world usage, SDK options, and best practices for secure and scalable automation. These APIs are essential for building infrastructure as code, embedding analytics into applications, and implementing DevOps and MLOps pipelines.

---

## Authentication for Azure APIs

All Azure REST APIs require authentication using **Azure Active Directory (Azure AD)**. The most common mechanisms include:

- **Client credentials flow** (client ID and secret)
- **Managed Identity** (VMs, Functions, Synapse)
- **Interactive login** (for testing via Postman or CLI)

### Token Retrieval (Client Credentials)

```
curl -X POST -H "Content-Type: application/x-www-form-urlencoded" \

-d
"grant_type=client_credentials&client_id=<client_id>&client_secret=<
\

"https://login.microsoftonline.com/<tenant_id>/oauth2/token"
```

Use the access_token from the response in the Authorization header for API calls.

---

## Azure Synapse Analytics APIs

### Management Endpoint:

```
https://management.azure.com/
subscriptions/{subscriptionId}/resourceGroups/{rg}/providers/
Microsoft.Synapse/
workspaces/{workspaceName}?api-version=2021-06-01
```

### Common Operations:

- Create workspace
- List and update SQL pools
- Manage Spark pools
- Trigger pipelines

**Sample: List All SQL Pools**

GET https://management.azure.com/subscriptions/{subId}/resourceGroups/{rg}/providers/Microsoft.Synapse/workspaces/{workspace}/sqlPools?api-version=2021-06-01

**Spark Job Submission:**

Use the dedicated endpoint:

https://{workspaceName}.dev.azuresynapse.net/livyApi/versions/2019-11-01-preview/sparkPools/{sparkPoolName}/batches

Payload Example:

{

"file": "abfss://scripts@storage.dfs.core.windows.net/spark-job.py",

"name": "MySparkJob",

"args": ["—input", "data.csv"]

}

---

## Azure Data Factory (ADF) APIs

**Management Endpoint:**

https://management.azure.com/subscriptions/{subId}/resourceGroups/{rg}/providers/Microsoft.DataFactory/factories/{factoryName}

**Key Functions:**

- Create/update pipelines
- Trigger pipeline runs
- Monitor pipeline status
- Get activity run logs

**Trigger a Pipeline Run:**

POST https://management.azure.com/subscriptions/{subId}/resourceGroups/{rg}/providers/Microsoft.DataFactory/factories/{factoryName}/pipelines/{pipelineName}/createRun?api-version

Optional body to pass parameters:

```
{
"ReferenceDate": "2024-12-01",
"DataSetType": "Incremental"
}
```

---

## Azure Data Lake Storage Gen2 REST API

**Endpoint Structure:**

https://<storageAccount>.dfs.core.windows.net/<filesystem>/<path>?res

**Operations:**

- Upload files
- Create/delete directories
- Read metadata
- Set ACLs and permissions

**Example: Upload a File**

PUT https://<storageAccount>.dfs.core.windows.net/filesystem/folder1/file1.txt

Headers:

Authorization: Bearer <token>

x-ms-version: 2020-08-04

x-ms-date: <timestamp>

Content-Type: text/plain

Use SAS tokens or OAuth 2.0 with Azure AD for secure access.

---

## Azure Machine Learning REST API

**Management Endpoint:**

https://management.azure.com/subscriptions/{subId}/resourceGroups/{rg}/providers/Microsoft.MachineLearningServices/workspaces/{workspaceName}

**Key Operations:**

- Submit training jobs
- Register models
- Deploy web services
- Monitor and update endpoints

**Deploy Model via REST:**

POST https://<region>.api.azureml.ms/modelmanagement/v1.0/subscriptions/{subId}/resourceGroups/{rg}/providers/Microsoft.MachineLearningServices/workspaces/{ws}/services

Payload Example:

{

"name": "churn-predictor",

"modelIds": ["churn_model:1"],

"computeType": "aci",

"description": "Churn classification model"

}

---

## Azure Purview API

Purview provides APIs to manage scans, classification rules, glossary terms, and metadata catalog.

**Base URL:**

https://{accountName}.purview.azure.com/catalog/api/

**Common Operations:**

- Create and retrieve assets
- Assign classifications
- Fetch lineage
- Manage glossary terms

**Get Lineage for Asset:**

GET https://{purviewAccount}.purview.azure.com/catalog/api/atlas/v2/lineage/{assetGuid}

**Create Glossary Term:**

POST https://{account}.purview.azure.com/catalog/api/atlas/v2/glossary/term

{

"name": "CustomerSegment",

"shortDescription": "Group of customers based on purchasing behavior"

}

---

## Azure Monitor and Log Analytics API

**Base Endpoint:**

https://api.loganalytics.io/v1/workspaces/{workspaceId}/query

**Example: Query Logs**

POST https://api.loganalytics.io/v1/workspaces/{workspaceId}/query

Headers:

Authorization: Bearer <token>

Body:

{

"query": "AzureDiagnostics | where ResourceType == 'DATAFACTORY'"

}

Used for retrieving metrics, custom logs, and diagnostics programmatically.

---

## SDKs and Language Support

Microsoft offers SDKs in multiple languages:

- **Python**: azure-mgmt-*, azure-ml-sdk, azure-identity, etc.
- **.NET / C#**: NuGet packages like Microsoft.Azure.Management.Synapse
- **Java**: Maven packages for Storage, Cosmos DB, etc.
- **JavaScript/TypeScript**: SDKs for client-side and Node.js usage
- **REST APIs**: For all services, REST endpoints are consistently available

Python Example: List Synapse Workspaces

from azure.identity import DefaultAzureCredential

```
from azure.mgmt.synapse import SynapseManagementClient

credential = DefaultAzureCredential()

client = SynapseManagementClient(credential,
"<subscription_id>")

for workspace in
client.workspaces.list_by_resource_group("my-rg"):

print(workspace.name)
```

---

## API Security and Throttling

When integrating APIs, keep in mind:

- Use **Key Vault** to manage secrets securely
- Apply **retry logic** for throttled requests (HTTP 429)
- Respect **rate limits** as documented in the official API specs
- Use **pagination** when retrieving large datasets
- Log every API call for **audit and troubleshooting**

---

## DevOps and CI/CD Integration

APIs are essential for automating deployments and testing. Integrate with:

- **GitHub Actions**
- **Azure DevOps Pipelines**

- **Terraform external data sources**
- **Logic Apps** (HTTP connector to call APIs)
- **PowerShell and CLI scripts**

---

## Summary

APIs are the connective tissue of the Azure data platform. Whether you're deploying infrastructure, automating ML workflows, ingesting streaming data, or managing metadata catalogs, the ability to interact with services programmatically unlocks powerful capabilities.

This guide serves as a reference to quickly start working with Azure's key data-related APIs. While REST endpoints remain the universal standard, using language-specific SDKs and managed identities can dramatically simplify and secure your implementations. Embrace APIs not only as a technical convenience but as a strategic enabler for agility, automation, and innovation.

# Frequently Asked Questions

This section addresses the most common questions and challenges faced by professionals working with Azure data services. These FAQs span architecture, tooling, governance, performance, cost, and career development. Whether you're just starting out or leading enterprise-scale data initiatives, this section aims to clarify key concepts, demystify common pain points, and help you avoid typical pitfalls.

---

## Architecture and Service Selection

**Q: Should I use Azure Synapse Analytics or Azure SQL Database for my data warehouse?**

**A:** Use **Azure Synapse** if you need massive scale, integrated Spark and SQL engines, and complex analytics across big data and structured sources. Use **Azure SQL** for transactional workloads or traditional data warehouse patterns at moderate scale. For enterprise analytics and integration, Synapse is generally more versatile.

**Q: When should I use Azure Data Lake vs. Azure Blob Storage?**

**A:** Use **Data Lake Storage Gen2** when working with big data, hierarchical folders, and analytics tools like Synapse, Spark, or Hadoop. Blob Storage is ideal for simpler object storage needs such as backups, documents, and web assets.

**Q: What's the difference between serverless and dedicated SQL pools in Synapse?**

**A:** Serverless SQL pools are on-demand and charge per query—ideal for ad hoc queries or infrequent use. Dedicated pools require provisioning and charge per DWU hour—better for consistent workloads, complex joins, and predictable performance.

---

## Data Integration and Pipelines

**Q: What's the difference between ADF Mapping Data Flows and Synapse Data Flows?**

**A:** Both support no-code ETL operations. Synapse Data Flows run inside Synapse pipelines and are better integrated with Spark pools. ADF Data Flows are more mature and provide broader activity support but live outside the Synapse environment.

**Q: How can I avoid duplicated pipeline runs in Data Factory?**

**A:** Use trigger concurrency limits and define idempotent logic in your activities. Store pipeline run states or hashes in a control table to prevent reprocessing.

**Q: Can I use Azure Data Factory to write to a REST API?**

**A:** Yes, using the **Web activity**. However, for complex API interactions (pagination, token renewal), consider integrating with **Azure Functions** or **Logic Apps** for enhanced control.

## Machine Learning and AI

**Q: How do I deploy an Azure ML model into Synapse Analytics?**

**A:** Convert your trained model to **ONNX** format and register it in Synapse using the PREDICT() T-SQL function, or deploy as a REST endpoint and call it from Synapse Notebooks or Pipelines.

**Q: Can I train machine learning models directly in Synapse?**

**A:** Yes. Synapse Spark pools support PySpark and MLlib for training models. For advanced experimentation, integrate with **Azure ML Studio** for better lifecycle and versioning support.

**Q: What's the difference between Cognitive Services and Azure ML?**

**A: Cognitive Services** are pre-trained APIs for common AI tasks (vision, language, speech). **Azure ML** is a full machine learning platform for building, training, and deploying custom models.

## Performance and Optimization

**Q: How can I reduce query latency in Synapse SQL Serverless?**

**A:** Optimize by:

- Querying partitioned files (Parquet/CSV) with folder pruning.
- Using external tables instead of OPENROWSET where possible.
- Minimizing wildcards and large scans.
- Using data types wisely to reduce cast operations.

**Q: Why is my ADF pipeline running slowly?**

**A:** Common reasons include:

- Under-provisioned Integration Runtimes.
- Data skew or inefficient Data Flows.
- Network latency between source and sink.
- Slow script activities with blocking transformations.

**Q: What's the best way to monitor Spark job performance in Synapse?**

**A:** Use the Spark Job Monitoring tab in Synapse Studio. Check for:

- Task skew
- Memory spills
- Shuffle operations Also enable verbose logging in Spark and consider using **Delta Lake** for transactional performance.

## Cost and Billing

**Q: How do I estimate Azure data service costs before deployment?**

**A:** Use the **Azure Pricing Calculator** to estimate costs for Synapse, ADF, SQL DB, Data Lake, etc. For more accuracy, combine with **Azure Cost Management + Billing** and set budgets with alerts.

**Q: What are some tips to reduce cost in Azure Synapse?**

**A:**

- Use serverless pools where possible.
- Pause dedicated pools when idle.
- Store data in Parquet.
- Avoid complex nested queries.
- Use **materialized views** for reused aggregations.

**Q: Can I get notified when my Azure bill goes over a threshold?**

**A:** Yes. Set **Budgets** in Azure Cost Management and configure alerts at specified thresholds (e.g., 80%, 100%).

---

## Security and Governance

**Q: How can I enforce RBAC across all my Synapse workspaces?**

**A:** Assign **Azure RBAC roles** at the subscription or resource group level (e.g., Synapse Contributor, Synapse Administrator). Use **Azure**

**Policy** to restrict resource creation to compliant regions or naming conventions.

**Q: What is the best way to manage secrets for pipelines and notebooks?**

**A:** Store credentials in **Azure Key Vault**, then reference them securely from Synapse, ADF, and Azure ML using linked services or managed identities.

**Q: Does Azure Synapse support private networking?**

**A:** Yes. Use **Managed Private Endpoints**, **Private Link**, and **NSGs** to keep all traffic within your virtual network.

---

## DevOps and Automation

**Q: Can I automate Synapse pipeline deployment with CI/CD?**

**A:** Yes. Use **Azure DevOps** or **GitHub Actions** to automate export/import of Synapse artifacts. Maintain JSON definitions in source control and deploy with ARM templates or REST APIs.

**Q: What tools are best for infrastructure as code (IaC)?**

**A:**

- **Bicep**: Native Azure IaC with strong tooling support.
- **Terraform**: Cloud-agnostic, widely adopted.
- **ARM Templates**: Powerful, but verbose.

**Q: How can I track changes to my data platform?**

**A:** Use:

- Git integration in Synapse Studio
- **Change tracking tables** in SQL
- **Purview lineage view**
- **Azure Monitor + Log Analytics** for audit and diagnostics

---

## Learning and Career

**Q: Which certifications should I pursue as a data professional?**

**A:**

- **DP-900**: Azure Data Fundamentals
- **DP-203**: Azure Data Engineer Associate
- **AI-900**: Azure AI Fundamentals
- **DP-420**: Azure Cosmos DB Developer

**Q: Are there sandbox environments to test without billing?**

**A:** Use **Microsoft Learn Sandbox** for hands-on modules. You can also activate a **Free Azure Account** with $200 credit.

**Q: How can I stay updated with new features?**

**A:** Subscribe to:

- Azure Updates:https://azure.microsoft.com/en-us/updates/
- Microsoft Tech Blogs

- GitHub repos for Azure SDKs and samples
- Azure Community YouTube Channels and newsletters

---

## Troubleshooting Common Issues

**Q: I can't see Synapse pipelines in Git—why?**

**A:** Ensure your workspace is linked to a Git repo and that you've committed your changes. Only published pipelines are visible in the Synapse Studio if Git integration is off.

**Q: Data Factory pipeline fails with a 403 error—what now?**

**A:** Check:

- Permissions on source/sink.
- Managed Identity access.
- Expired linked service credentials.
- VNet rules if private endpoint is used.

**Q: Spark jobs keep failing due to OOM (Out of Memory)—how to fix?**

**A:**

- Increase driver and executor memory.
- Optimize data partitions.
- Avoid Cartesian joins and UDF misuse.
- Monitor job diagnostics and scale accordingly.

## Summary

These frequently asked questions reflect real-world challenges faced by Azure data practitioners. From choosing the right architecture to securing your pipeline and controlling costs, this section provides rapid, actionable answers that help accelerate your decision-making.

As Azure continues to evolve, revisit this FAQ regularly and consider contributing to the broader community through blog posts, forums, and shared GitHub repositories. The more we learn and share, the stronger and more agile our data ecosystems become.

www.ingramcontent.com/pod-product-compliance
Lightning Source LLC
LaVergne TN
LVHW090257210926
848480LV00001B/52